THE ART OF
XCOM 2

THE ART OF

Introduction by
GREG FOERTSCH

TITAN BOOKS

An Insight Editions Book

CONTENTS

WELKOM TO KITYKIGHTKR
A KITY OF BEAUTY, THE HEART OF FUTURE

INTRODUCTION

BY GREG FOERTSCH
XCOM 2 PROJECT ART DIRECTOR

When we first embarked upon creating the *XCOM: Enemy Unknown* universe, our goal was to create an immersive world populated by heroes that inspired, aliens that played off of UFO lore, and environments that were familiar and resonated with the player. These ideas remained at the core of the visual direction for *XCOM 2*. But balancing the familiar with the fantastic was the biggest challenge we faced in establishing a world set in a dystopian future. As the concept art started to pile up, the vision became clearer, and we began to see the future and embrace the world of 2035.

The clean, slick, and reflective look of the ADVENT cities and a world of alien rule brought some new challenges with them that ultimately impacted the visual direction of the game. The unique look of *XCOM* is that of a stylized realism that relies on form, color, and cameras that all work together. With *XCOM 2*, we needed to retain that unique look while increasing the fidelity and depth of the art. We wanted to improve the player experience through higher-resolution character models, more robust animation, and materials that physically represent the world in new ways. The goal was to create an immersive world for the player, enhanced by game cameras that not only provide exciting visual opportunities but also reinforce the information the game is trying to convey. The game models live in a space where the forms are slightly chunky yet clean in silhouette; the color is pushed to help create mood and atmosphere; and the animation is clean and fluid, with a slight overemphasis on the action to help make it distinctive from multiple viewing angles.

Looking back at the project, it is impossible to share in full the countless concepts, iterations, and trials we went through to find just the right look that satisfies both the art and design visions. The vision we landed on is one that is clearly based in reality yet is inspired by the feel of action figures and miniatures. From the earliest days of preproduction, this was the direction we were striving for, but it evolved and strengthened from the first game to the second. The amazing thing about the look of any game is that each artist contributes to the direction—grows it, expands it, and defines it. It transcends the person who started the specific piece and eventually evolves into the team's vision.

Every day I walk through the halls and offices of Firaxis, and every day seems more exciting than the last. I feel privileged to have seen all of the art that contributed to the ideas that have evolved and led to the final vision. The art in this book is only a fraction of what was generated throughout the development of *XCOM 2*. So much energy goes into this work, but so few people get to see because it doesn't make it into final game. This book is a chance to let you into the process, to provide a glimpse of all the tremendous behind-the-scenes efforts of my amazingly talented team. We hope you enjoy and appreciate it as much as we have.

CHAPTER 1

PREVISUALIZATION

The previsualization team at Firaxis Games began working on the XCOM sequel shortly after the expansion to the critically acclaimed *XCOM: Enemy Unknown* was released. Led by art director Greg Foertsch, the small team set out to crystalize a specific art style unique to this futuristic vision of an alien-controlled Earth, taking place twenty years after the events of the last game.

"When the aliens showed up, XCOM suffered massive casualties, and governments around the world crumbled in the face of popular support to surrender," explains creative director Jake Solomon. "Then, Earth was quickly overrun. So twenty years into the future, the world is a very different place. The aliens rule Earth from giant, shining megacities which all the people of Earth are flocking. That's where they're promised an easy life—a secure life free of disease."

The previs team's goal was to determine the key details of the game—anything from the appropriate camera angles and the right effects to the ways the enemy reacts to the player. They were tasked with creating a good working model for what the game was eventually going to look like—as well as generating excitement about the dynamic potentials of a world where powerful aliens have taken over our cities, while a ragtag band of fighters continue to fight the good fight against occupation.

As senior concept artist Piero Macgowan explains, "Seeing things come to life in those beginning stages is an exciting experience for us. Moving forward to the next level of visual fidelity, discovering the new aliens and weapons—these are aspects of the game that keep us all very engaged."

Senior concept artist Aaron Yamada-Hanff agrees: "You are working with these broad concepts, so you try out hundreds of different things. There are technical restrictions that you deal with, but you keep pushing to make something work. You try to convey the right mood, get the material right, deliver the right mix of shadows and color—and, then suddenly, the whole thing comes alive and finds a life of its own."

One of the main challenges the previs artists faced was how to push the envelope visually to satisfy the original game's discerning fan base. They knew they had to add a multitude of flourishes and come up with new thrills and surprises to keep the players on their toes.

As Yamada-Hanff points out, "Some of the concepts we were toying with could not be translated into the game because of the unique features of the grid that *XCOM* is based on. We had to learn to use the right 3-D tools to work with it rather than against it."

The sequel's new soldier classes with their unique skill sets and complex enemies such as female Vipers, ADVENT soldiers, and evolved Sectoids are only a few of the new elements the Firaxis team explores in this adventure. More flexible tactical combat, the ability to upgrade weapon and armors, the introduction of stealth-infused strategies to defeat enemies, procederally-generated maps, and technology to empower the secret force are just some of the undeniable thrills of *XCOM 2.*

PAGES 12–13: A high-resolution render from the initial previsualization movie. **OPPOSITE:** Key art shows how the team envisioned the hazy, neon-lit City Centers as panopticon-like prisons, with ADVENT lasers scanning the streets.

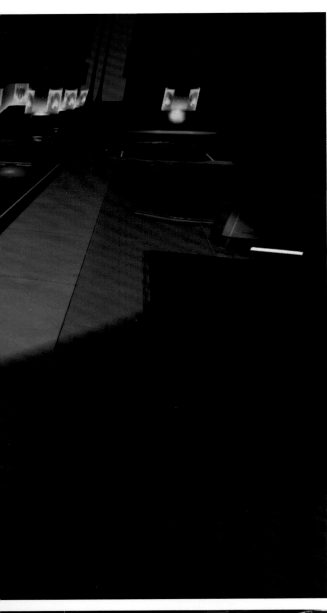

"We had to learn to work with the grid rather than against it by using 3-D tools. The grid really helped us with the design of the futuristic City Center, but it was harder to work with it for our rural environments because it had to look haphazard in the wilderness." —PIERO MACGOWAN, SENIOR CONCEPT ARTIST

LEFT: This previsualization of the map-building process helped to establish the look of City Centers. **OPPOSITE BOTTOM:** Final renders from the cinematic sequence. **BELOW:** A concept showing the props and materials for the City Center previsualization cinematic.

STRUCTURE IS
128 UNITS HIGH
HIGH COVER / PART OF

SOLAR AC / PLANTER

THESE PAGES: Map-building process art shows
the range of features that could be used for cover
in City Centers—from solar-powered planters to
media towers, medians, and light panels.

MEDIA/INFORMATION TOWERS

'DRIVERLESS' CAR SENSORS

MEDIAN

UNDERLYING BUILDING STRUCTURE BEHIND GLASS FOR COVER

TOUCHSCREEN INTERACTIVE DISPLAYS

PLEXI LIGHT PANELS

ABOVE: Process work shows the gruesome ADVENT torture chamber. **RIGHT AND OPPOSITE BOTTOM:** The torture bed. **OPPOSITE TOP:** A range of torture devices adhere to the table via a magnet located under the glass.

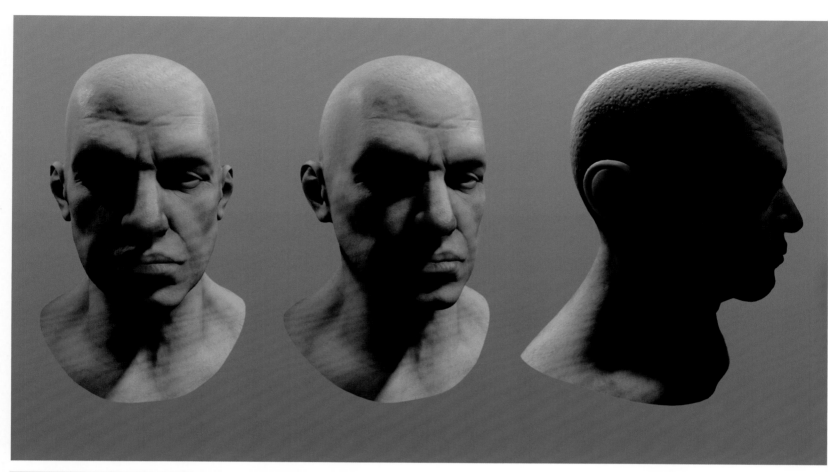

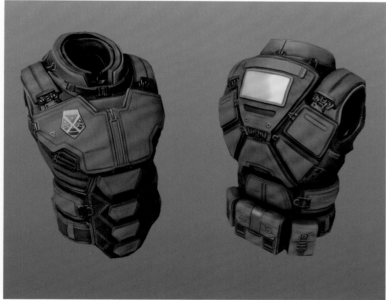

TOP: The visual target for soldier facial and head designs in chiaroscuro. **ABOVE AND RIGHT:** Shader development shows tinting being refined in early material design. **OPPOSITE:** Early development work used to explore a range of facial caricatures.

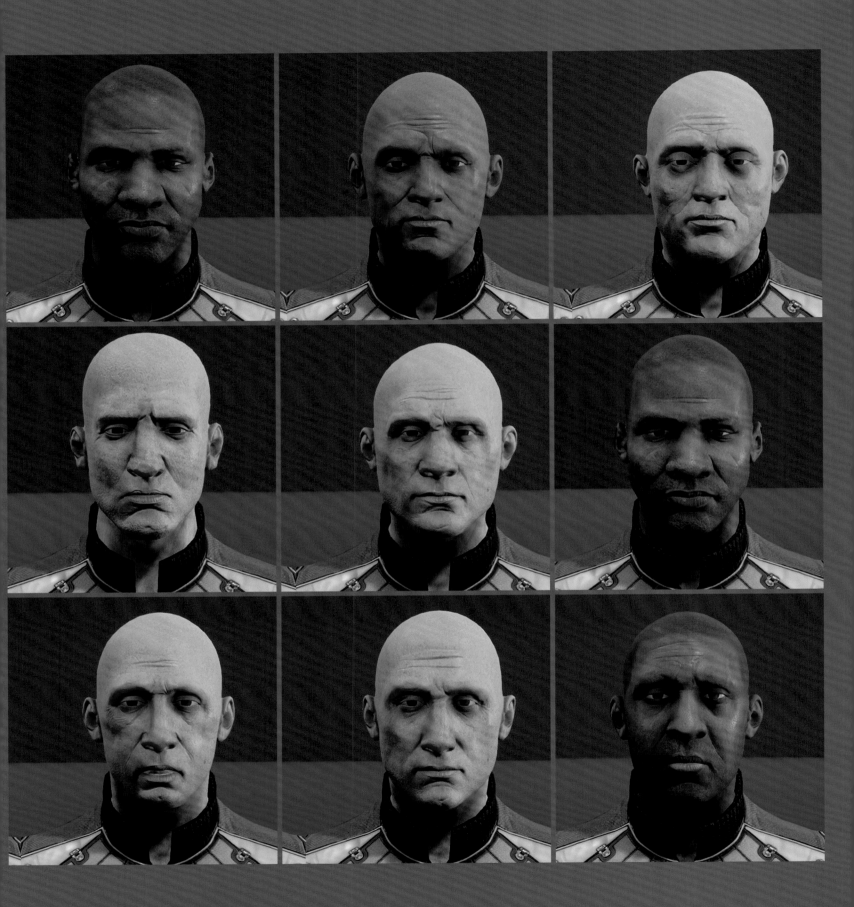

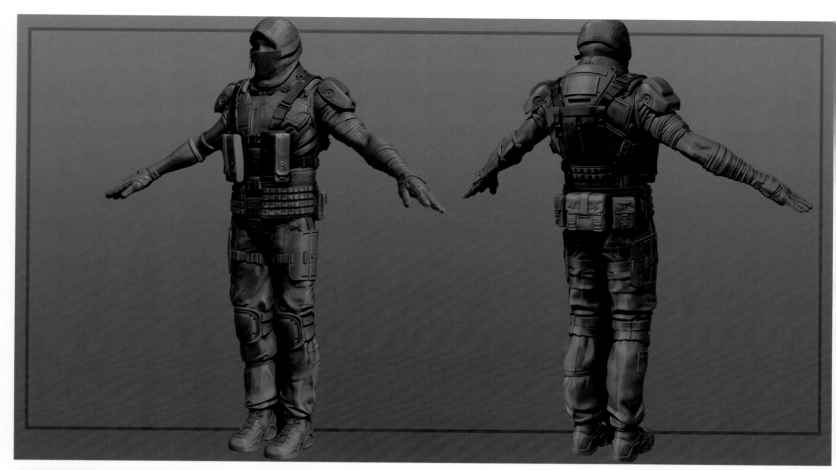

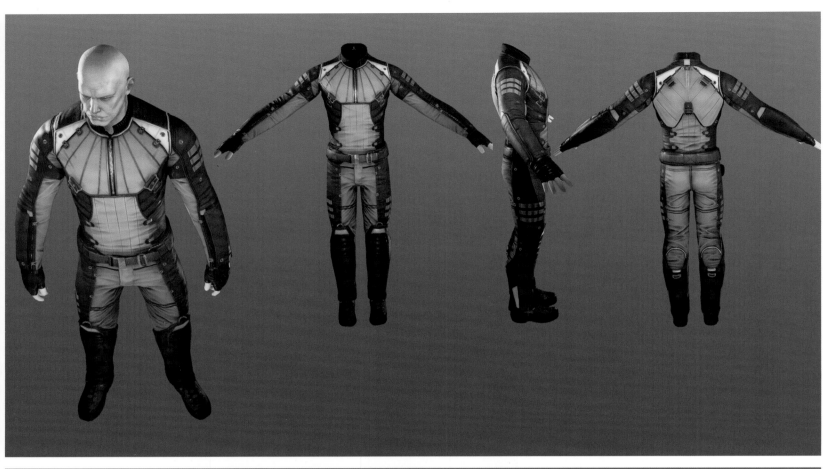

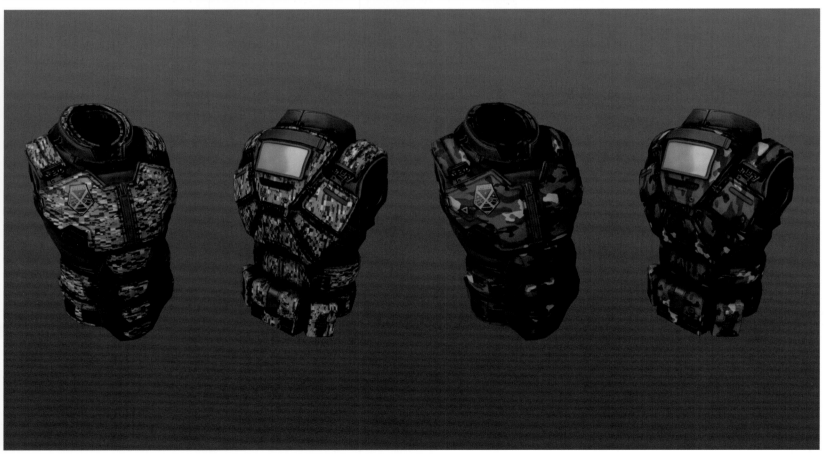

OPPOSITE TOP: A high-resolution model for conventional XCOM armor. **OPPOSITE BOTTOM:** An in-engine render of the baseline conventional armor. **TOP:** Base uniform and underlay for XCOM soldiers. **ABOVE:** The first example of armor patterns working in-game.

OPPOSITE TOP: High-resolution model. **OPPOSITE BOTTOM:** High resolution render of the Andromedon. **LEFT:** An early rough mass drawing of the Andromedon was used as a guide for the high-resolution model (*opposite top*).

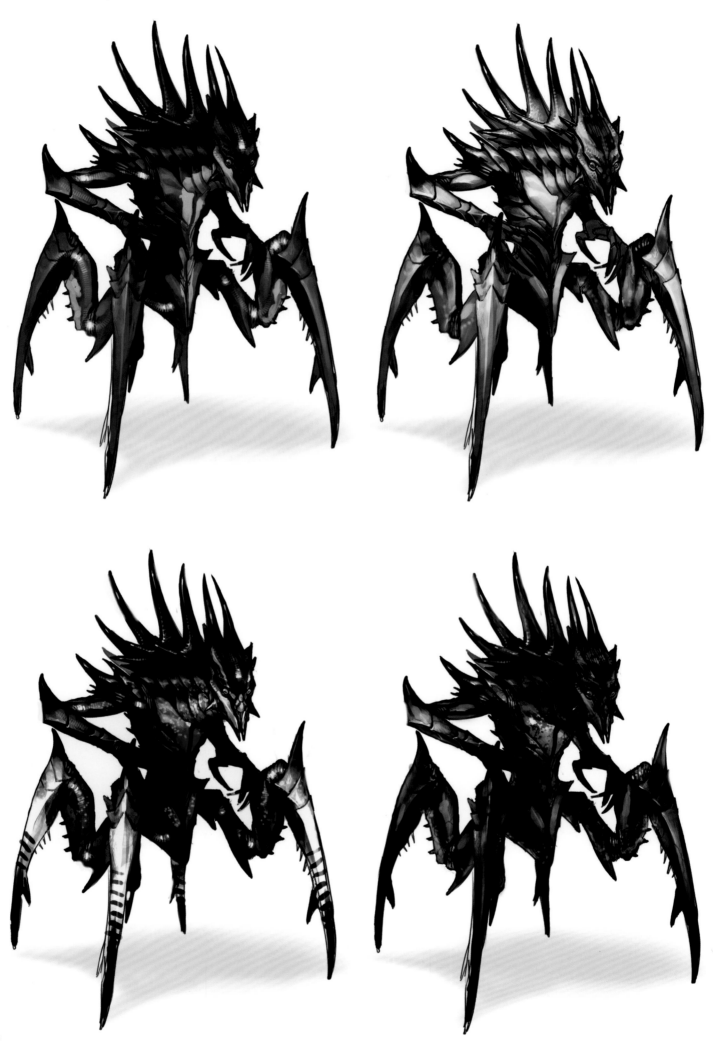

THESE PAGES: A range of color options were explored for the Chryssalid before settling on the speckled patterns seen in game.

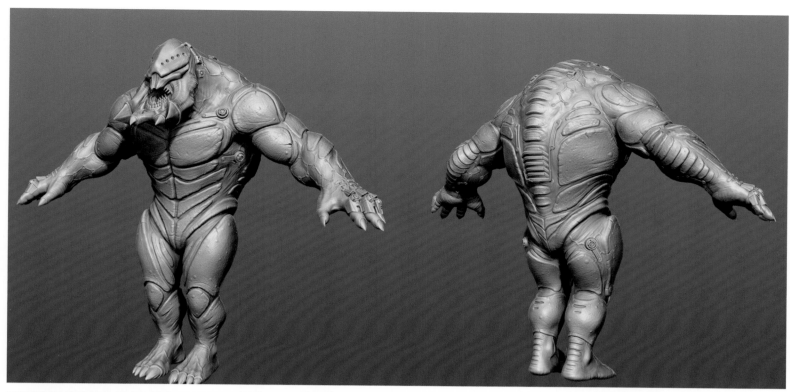

OPPOSITE TOP: A high-resolution Berserker model shows the unit's armor system. Berserker armor is genetically engineered to be a part of her skin. **OPPOSITE BOTTOM:** Game-resolution Berserker model. **THIS PAGE:** Early renders of the Muton model.

BEATDOWN

THESE PAGES: Animation concept sheet for the Berserker's "beat down" ability.

33

ENVIRONMENTS

Despite that *XCOM: Enemy Unknown* featured more than eighty handcrafted maps, one of the most common fan requests was to have more environments and maps added to the next installment, and the artists and designers at Firaxis were happy to oblige. The gleaming city centers built by the aliens for the humans (such as New Providence in the year 2035), the rural areas where humans seek refuge from total alien control, and the climate-specific regions known as biomes (desert, temperate, tundra, etc.) are among the key visually striking backdrops ready for exploration in the sequel.

The development team also set out to create an almost infinite variety of environments by producing components that can be built within the game procedurally, providing players territory to explore and fight over. Among the major technical achievements of the sequel is the fact that assets can be built and switched around in the different biomes. While each space conforms to the general rules and follows a unifying art style, they can also look vastly different from each other, thanks to the variety of terrains available.

The procedurally generated settings also play an important role in the players' secondary mission objectives. "It might be blowing up one of the buildings to spark the resistance," says art director Greg Foertsch. "Or it might be hacking a workstation or protecting a device. All these different things you can do that can show up in dozens of different buildings and areas. And you don't know what you're going to get."

Thanks to Firaxis' new system, players get maps that drastically change each time they encounter them, drawing from a large pool of components such as buildings, roads, and different types of terrain to create battlefields that look fantastic and are more destructible than ever. Foertsch says because the maps are procedurally generated, the AI has been modified to allow aliens to navigate and fight on them.

While *XCOM 2* offers its own distinct visual style, the artists also found inspiration by observing real-life landscapes and objects. PBR (Physically Based Rendering) technology allowed them to closely replicate patterns of reflection and absorption as seen in real-world objects.

As lead technical artist Zeljko Strkalj points out, "Because we began the project using PBR, everyone worked really hard to push the visuals harder, and we were very proud of the look we were able to achieve." He adds, "This switch to PBR makes the game look a bit more realistic. Surfaces are more recognizable. It really complements our artistic style and manages to look both heroic and real at the same time. It's great eye candy and really meets the high standards of modern game development."

Sharp observers may also notice hidden Easter Eggs and nods to the previous installments of the series randomly scattered in the environments. "You might see some familiar faces in a holographic poster," says Strkalj. "Or an enemy sprite might pop up on an arcade cabinet. It's all part of the playful, creative spirit we try to maintain as we work on these challenging games."

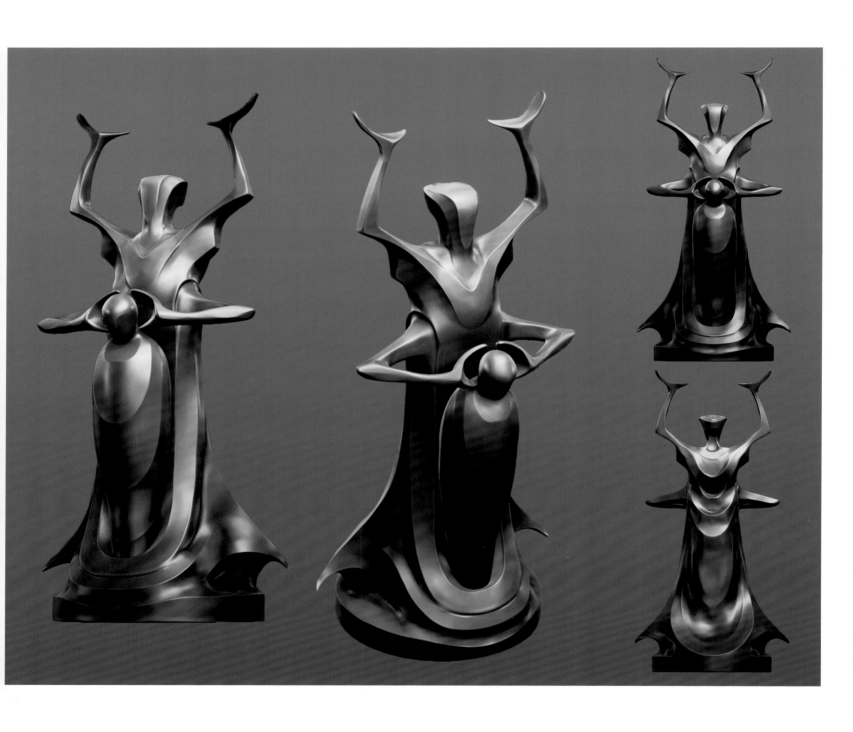

PAGES 38–39: A visualization of the City Center at night shows the streets rendered blue by ADVENT notices on the omnipresent light panels. **THESE PAGES:** Alien propaganda statues for City Centers depict tributes to the Elders.

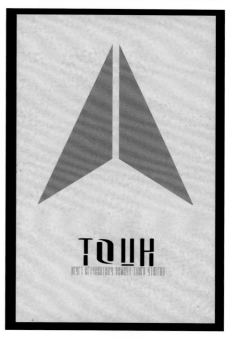

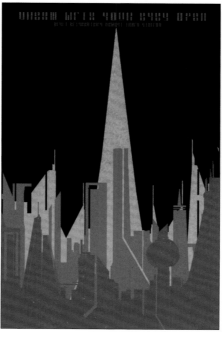

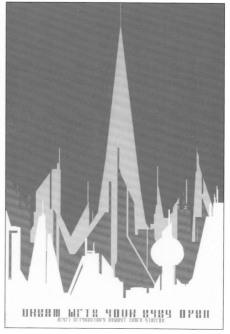

DREAM WITH YOUR EYES OPEN

OPPOSITE AND TOP: Explorations of the propaganda signage used to draw humans to the City Centers. **ABOVE:** Resistance and XCOM graffiti and symbols rendered in black spray paint. **FOLLOWING PAGES:** Two ADVENT propaganda posters.

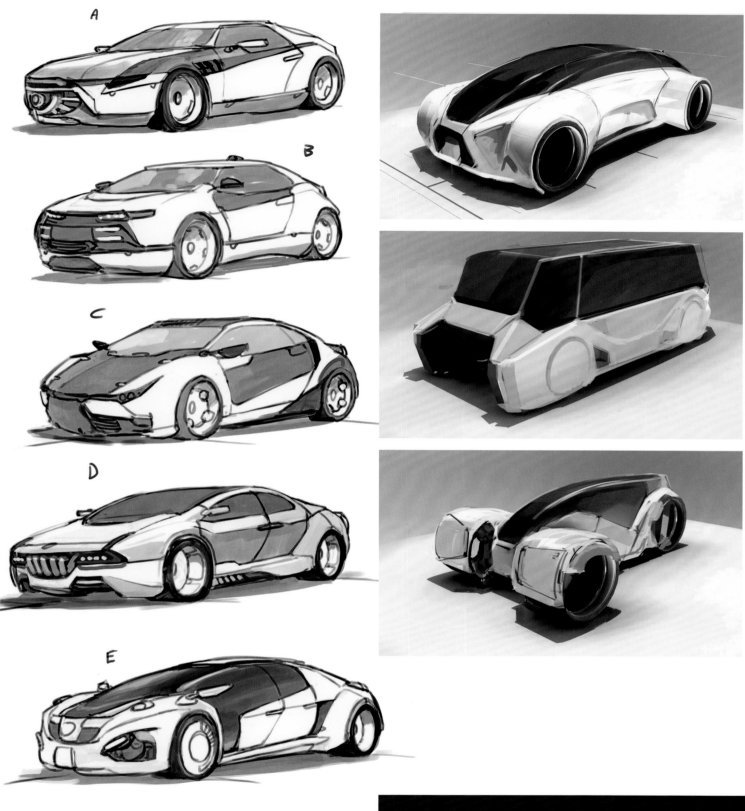

A

B

C

D

E

THIS PAGE: Concepts for City Center vehicles show how the artists smoothed and shrunk earlier designs. **OPPOSITE:** High-resolution models of some of the vehicles in City Center.

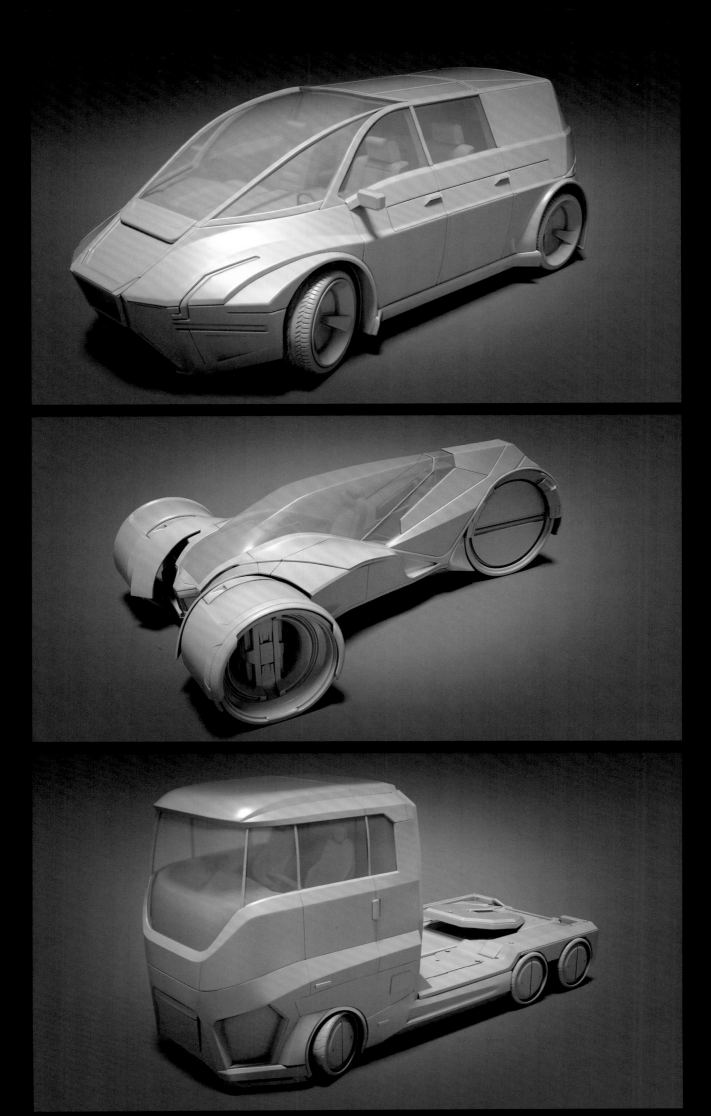

PROGRESS THROUGH COOPERA

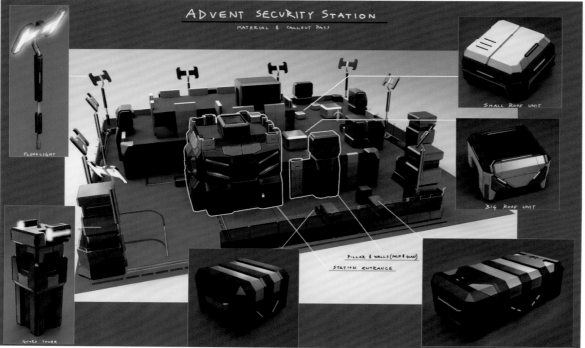

ADVENT SECURITY STATION
MATERIAL & CALLOUT PASS

FLOODLIGHT

SMALL ROOF UNIT

BIG ROOF UNIT

GUARD TOWER

PILLAR & WALLS (SOLID & GLASS)
STATION ENTRANCE

PREVIOUS PAGES: An ADVENT security checkpoint at night. **ABOVE:** A City Center stage area prepared for public propaganda speeches and gatherings. **LEFT:** A Concept for an ADVENT security station. **OPPOSITE:** Concepts for (*top to bottom*) ADVENT brig/jail cells, ADVENT VIP rooms, and ADVENT checkpoints.

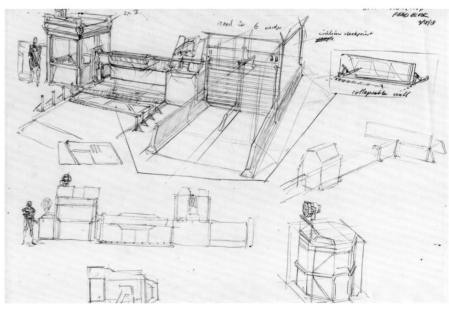

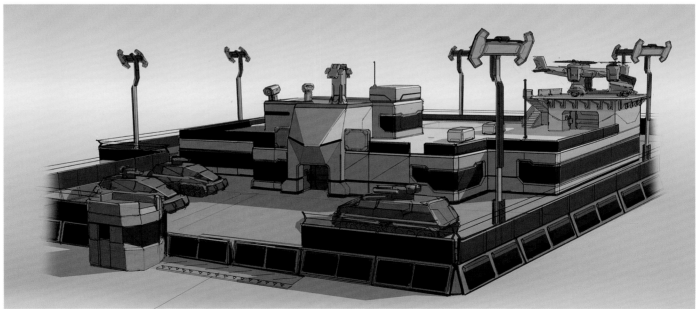

TOP: Concept art for the interior of ADVENT buildings shows a smooth, metallic motif illuminated in red. **ABOVE:** An early, rough concept for an ADVENT security station. **OPPOSITE TOP:** Concept of the ADVENT desk and lobby wall. **OPPOSITE BOTTOM:** Concepts for an ADVENT soldier rejuvenation chamber.

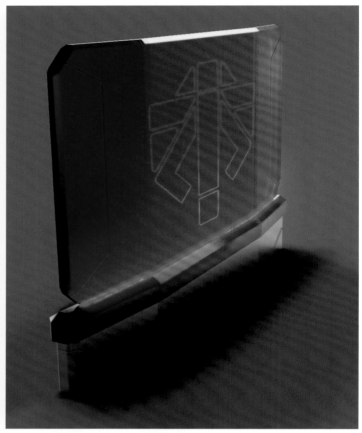

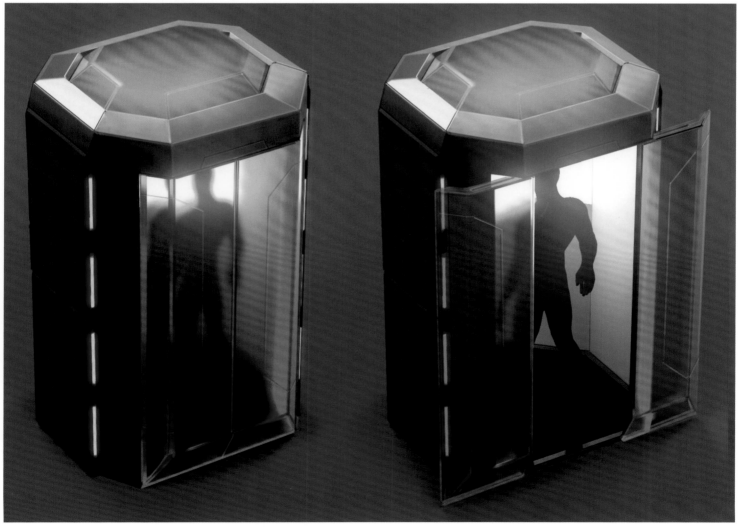

128

8 UNITS

2 TILES

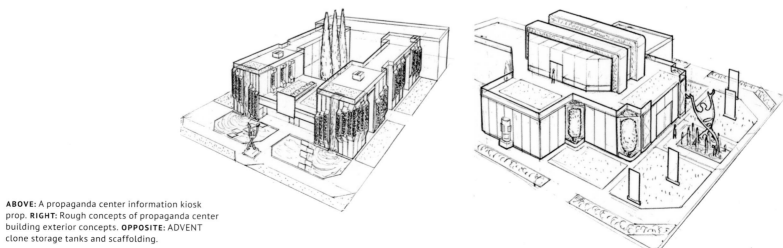

ABOVE: A propaganda center information kiosk prop. **RIGHT:** Rough concepts of propaganda center building exterior concepts. **OPPOSITE:** ADVENT clone storage tanks and scaffolding.

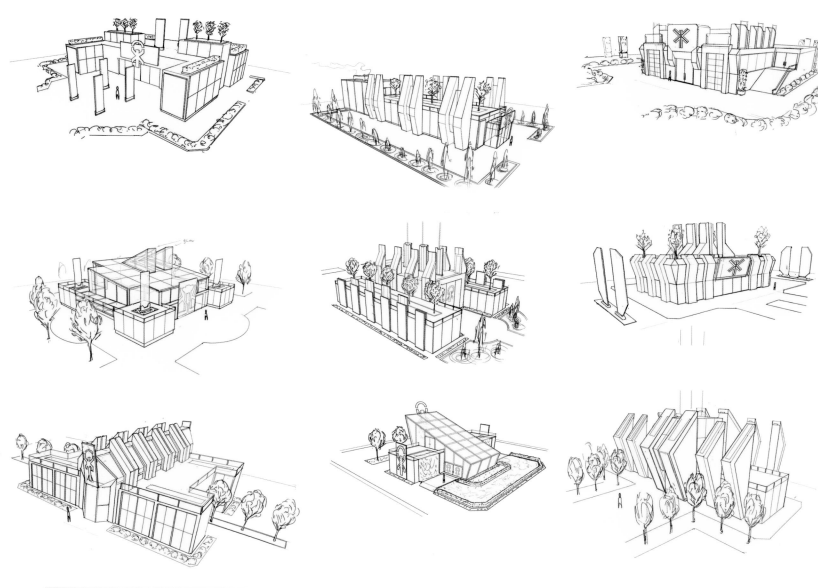

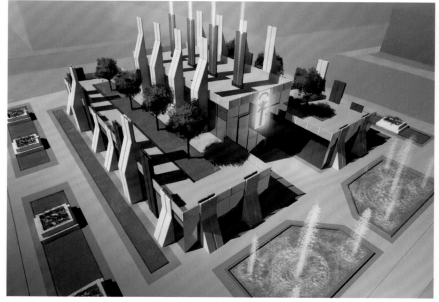

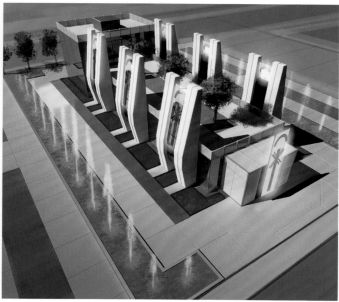

TOP: Rough concepts for the exteriors of propaganda centers showcase a cathedral-like design. **ABOVE:** Final concept work for the propaganda center's exteriors. **OPPOSITE:** Interior concepts of the propaganda center's side room (*opposite top*) and main room (*opposite bottom*).

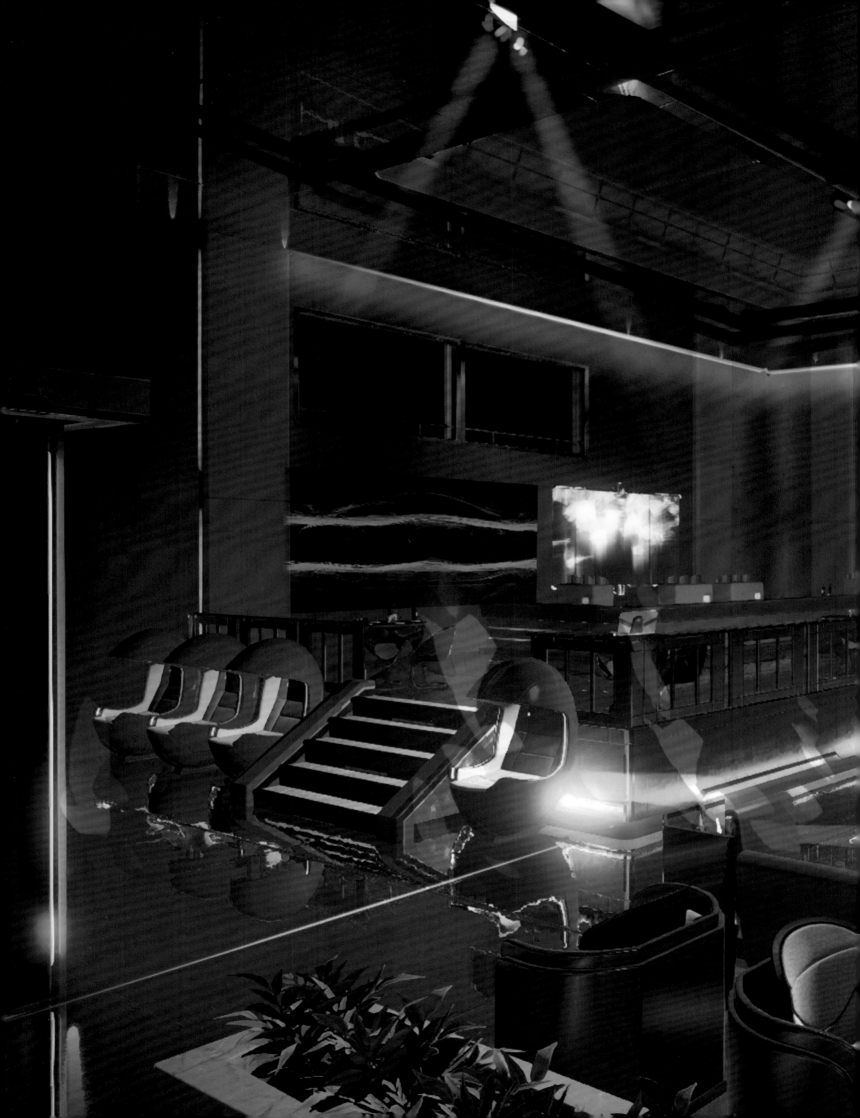

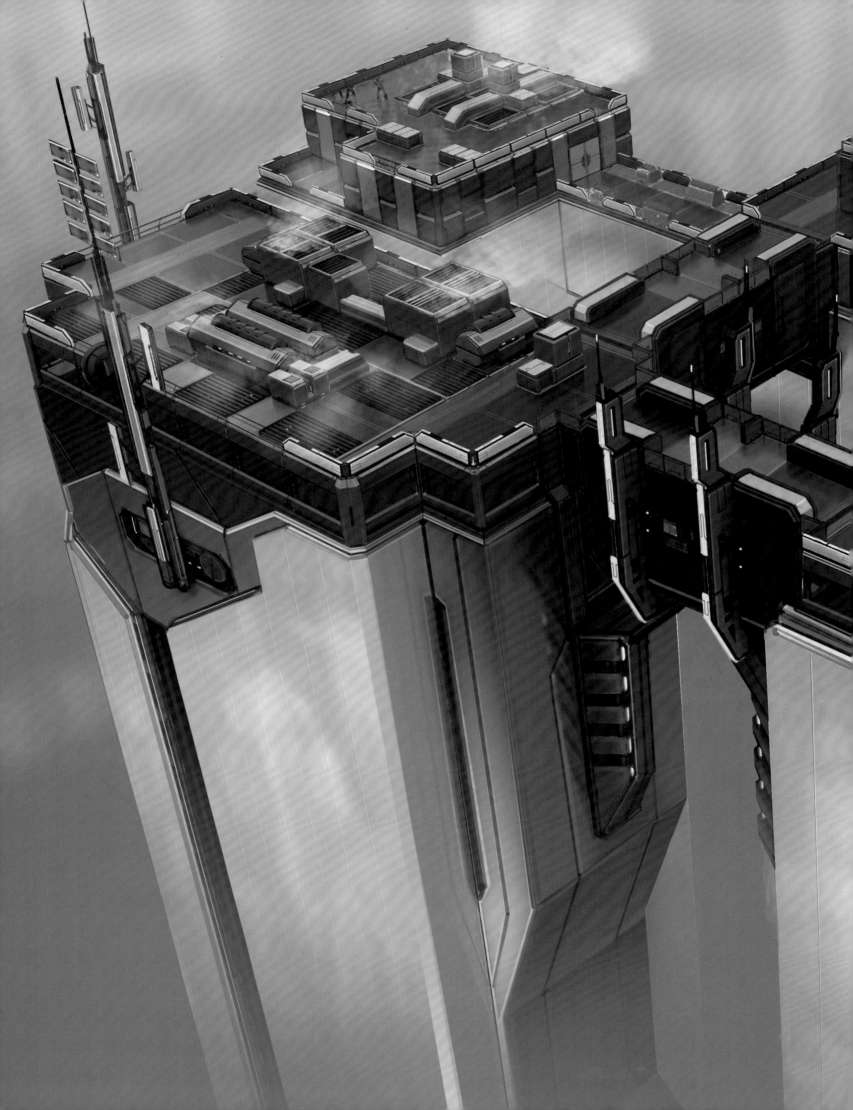

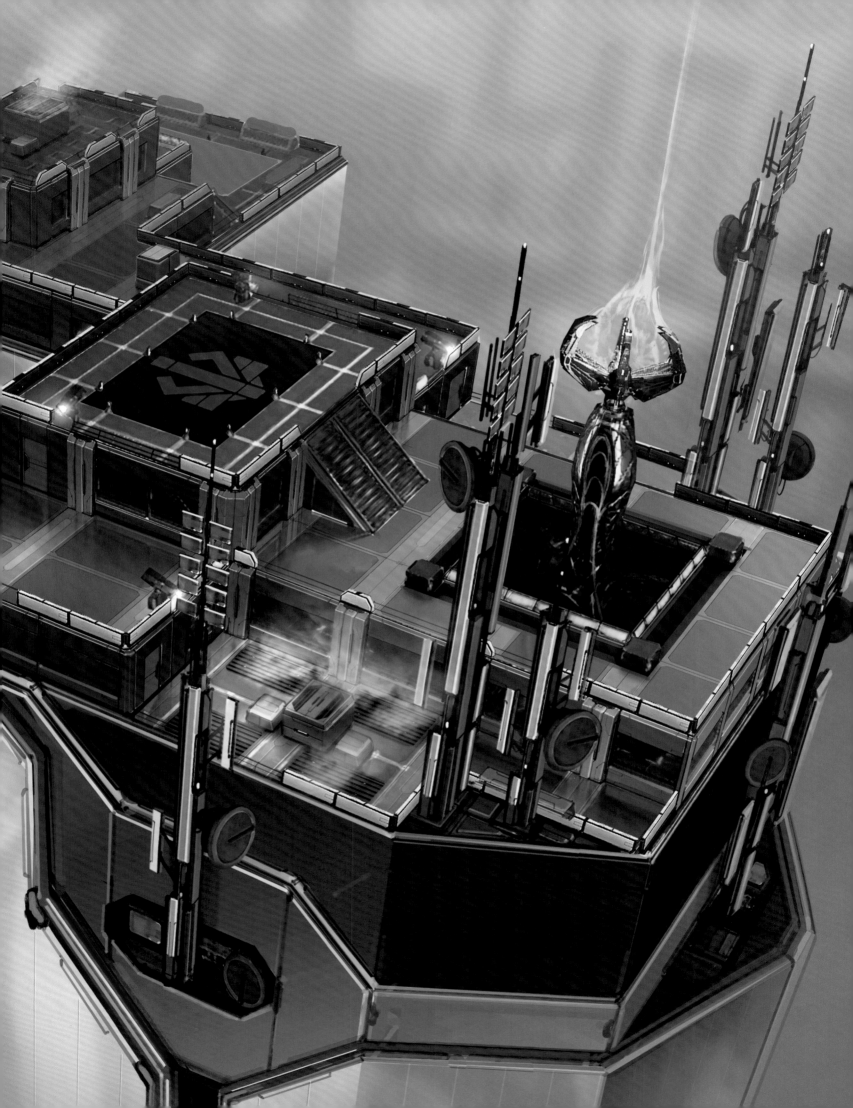

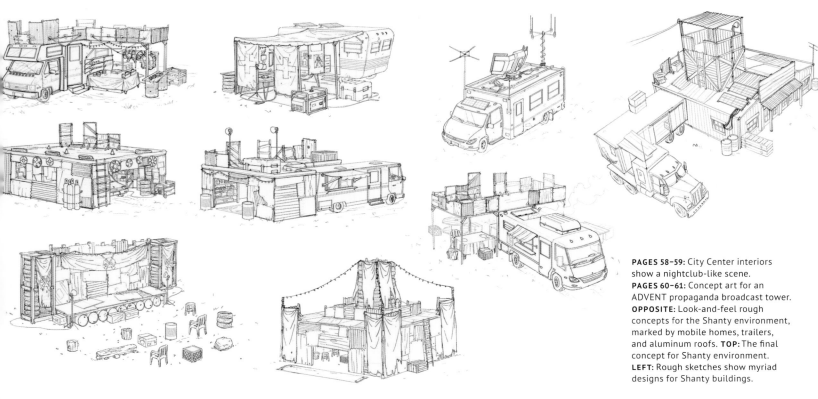

PAGES 58-59: City Center interiors show a nightclub-like scene.
PAGES 60-61: Concept art for an ADVENT propaganda broadcast tower.
OPPOSITE: Look-and-feel rough concepts for the Shanty environment, marked by mobile homes, trailers, and aluminum roofs. **TOP:** The final concept for Shanty environment.
LEFT: Rough sketches show myriad designs for Shanty buildings.

PREVIOUS PAGES: Concept art for the Small Town environment. ABOVE: Interior concepts for a Small Town house strewn with belongings. LEFT: Concept showing how destructible floors, roofs, and walls would smolder and burn if damaged sufficiently. OPPOSITE TOP: Small Town environment props show a range of power sources and communications equipment. OPPOSITE CENTER: A backyard concept shows a surprisingly tranquil patio area. OPPOSITE BOTTOM: Small Town house look-and-feel concept with alternative energy sources.

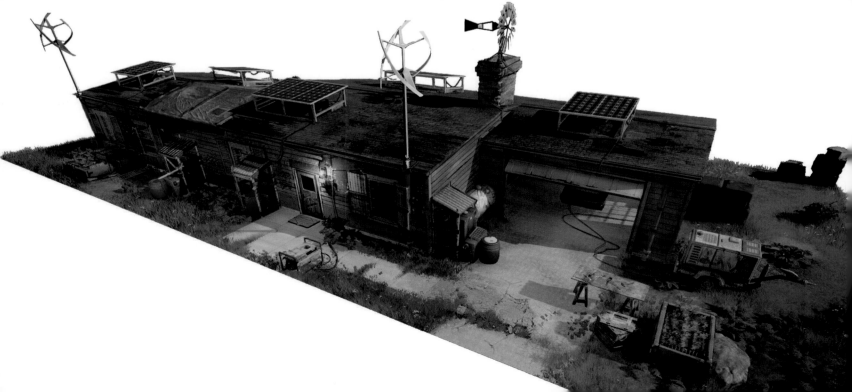

TOP: A diner overgrown and shuttered, with an alternate-energy vehicle parked out front.
OPPOSITE BOTTOM: Interior view of the overgrown diner.
LEFT: An overgrown gas station.

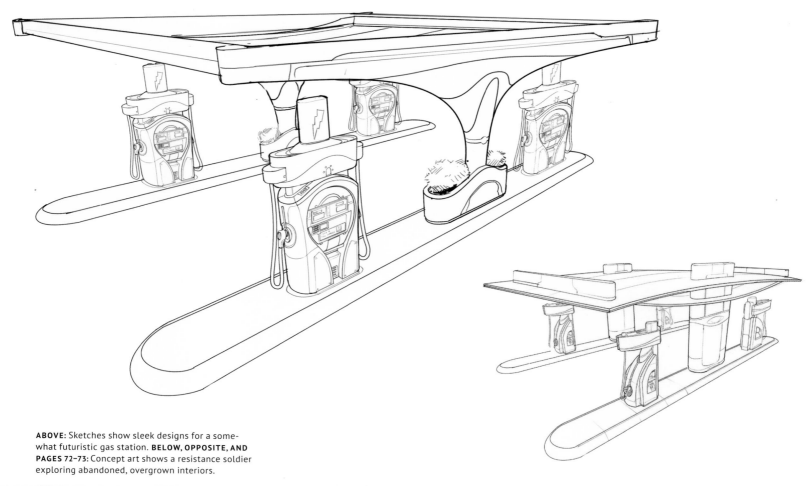

ABOVE: Sketches show sleek designs for a somewhat futuristic gas station. **BELOW, OPPOSITE, AND PAGES 72–73:** Concept art shows a resistance soldier exploring abandoned, overgrown interiors.

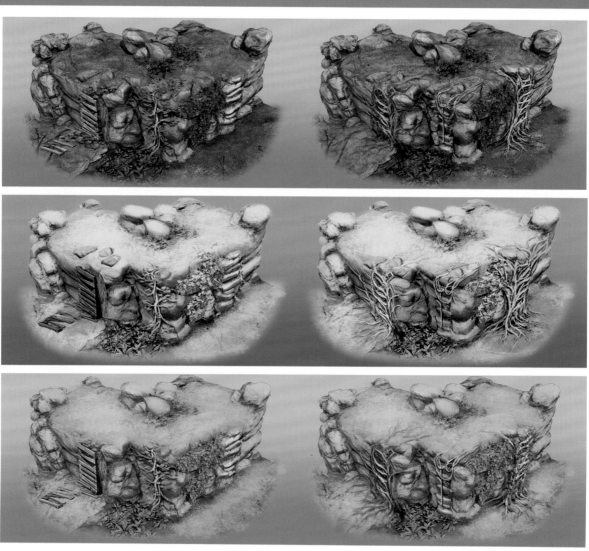

"We have a lot of foliage in our game, so we needed a quick way to vertex paint all that geometry to stay grounded according to wind strength and storm intensity. I wrote a script to work with those objects and enable them to interact with the wind so that when we have intense stormy weather in the game, the grass or the trees shake according to the strength and direction of the wind, just as it would in real life." —ZELJKO STRKALJ, LEAD TECHNICAL ARTIST

OPPOSITE TOP: A handful of the arid foliage and cover props used by the procedural level system. **OPPOSITE BOTTOM:** Wilderness ladders and plateaus acquire different details depending on the biome. **TOP:** Procedural level concepts covering wilderness biomes Temperate, Arid, and Tundra. **ABOVE:** Tundra tree concepts show a variety of foliage.

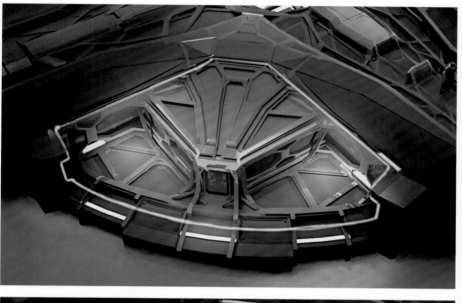

THESE PAGES: A series of concepts for the UFO's exterior, including designs for the corner structure within the energy field (*opposite top*) and the energy field's exteriors (*opposite center*).

Autopsy

Nav

ALIEN UFO: ROOM BLOCK-IN ROUGHS
XCOM II / 4.22.15

Powercore

OPPOSITE: Concept art for
UFO rooms, one intended for
autopsies (*top*) and one for
navigation purposes (*bottom*).
TOP: A UFO block-in with roof
cutaway was used to consider
modular parts, in order to
generate a variety of possible
layouts. LEFT: The UFO's power
core and central hub.

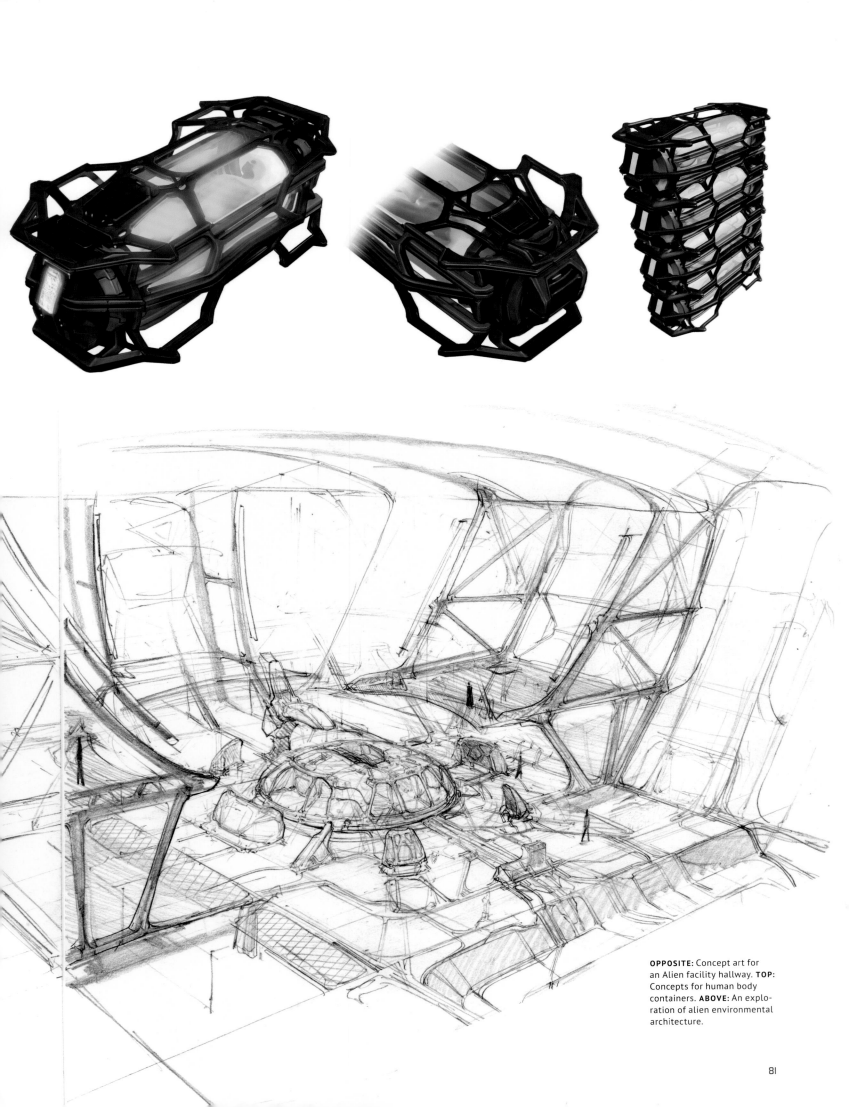

OPPOSITE: Concept art for an Alien facility hallway. **TOP:** Concepts for human body containers. **ABOVE:** An exploration of alien environmental architecture.

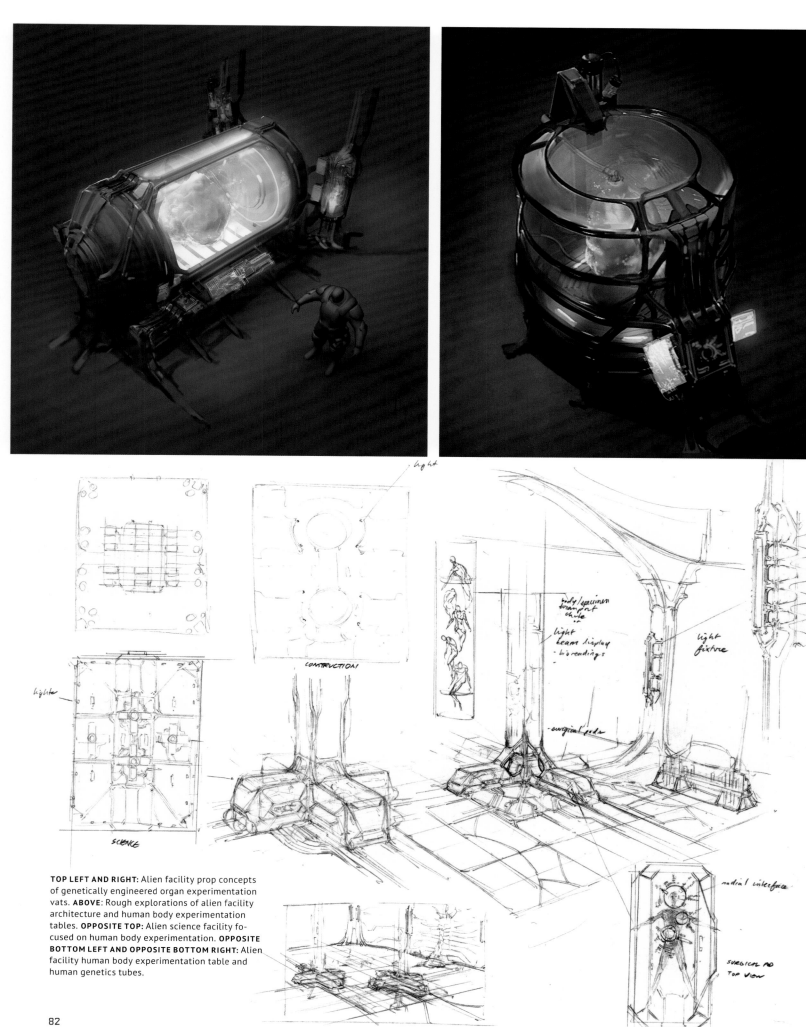

TOP LEFT AND RIGHT: Alien facility prop concepts of genetically engineered organ experimentation vats. **ABOVE:** Rough explorations of alien facility architecture and human body experimentation tables. **OPPOSITE TOP:** Alien science facility focused on human body experimentation. **OPPOSITE BOTTOM LEFT AND OPPOSITE BOTTOM RIGHT:** Alien facility human body experimentation table and human genetics tubes.

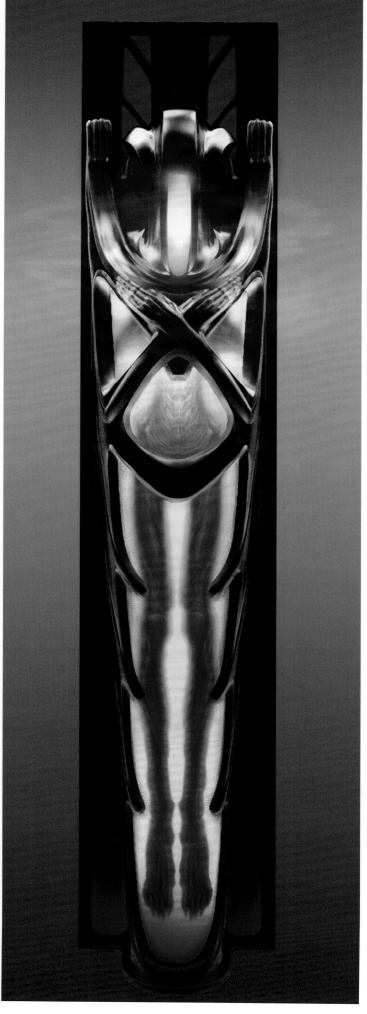

THESE PAGES: Ethereal sarcophagus roughs and concept art.

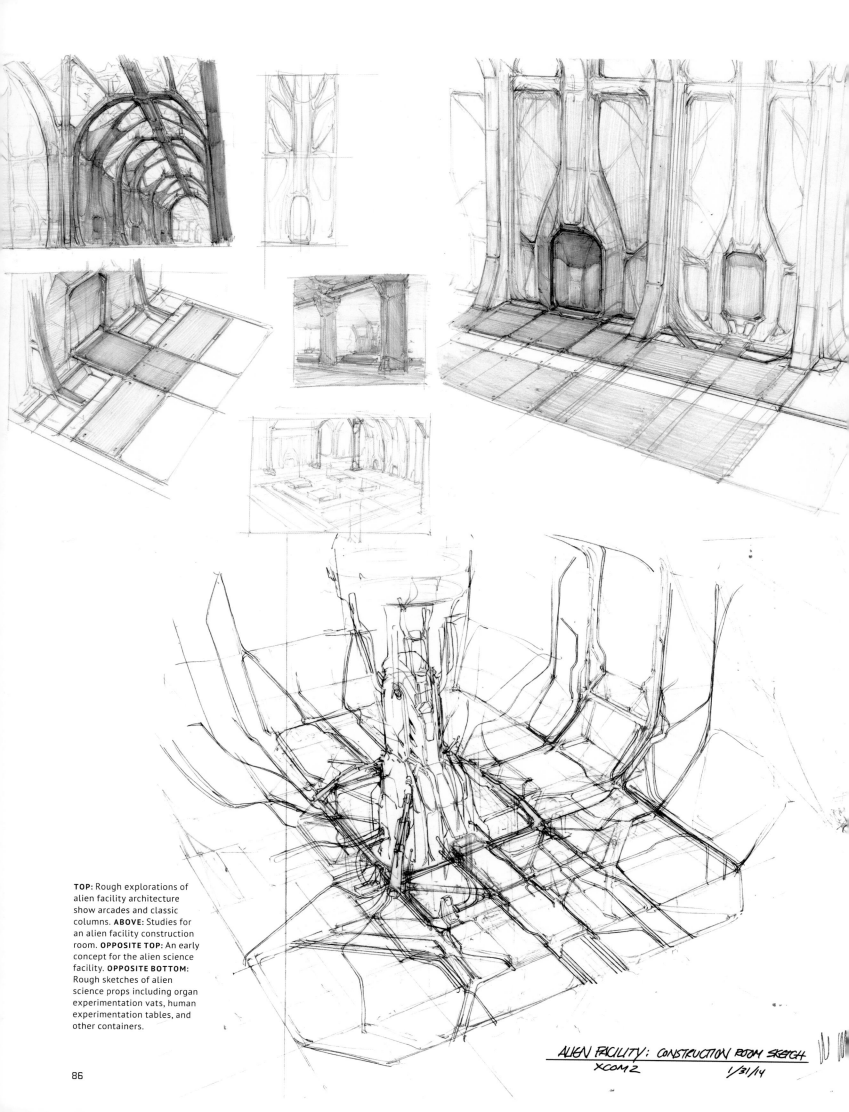

TOP: Rough explorations of alien facility architecture show arcades and classic columns. **ABOVE:** Studies for an alien facility construction room. **OPPOSITE TOP:** An early concept for the alien science facility. **OPPOSITE BOTTOM:** Rough sketches of alien science props including organ experimentation vats, human experimentation tables, and other containers.

ALIEN FACILITY: CONSTRUCTION ROOM SKETCH
XCOM2   1/31/14

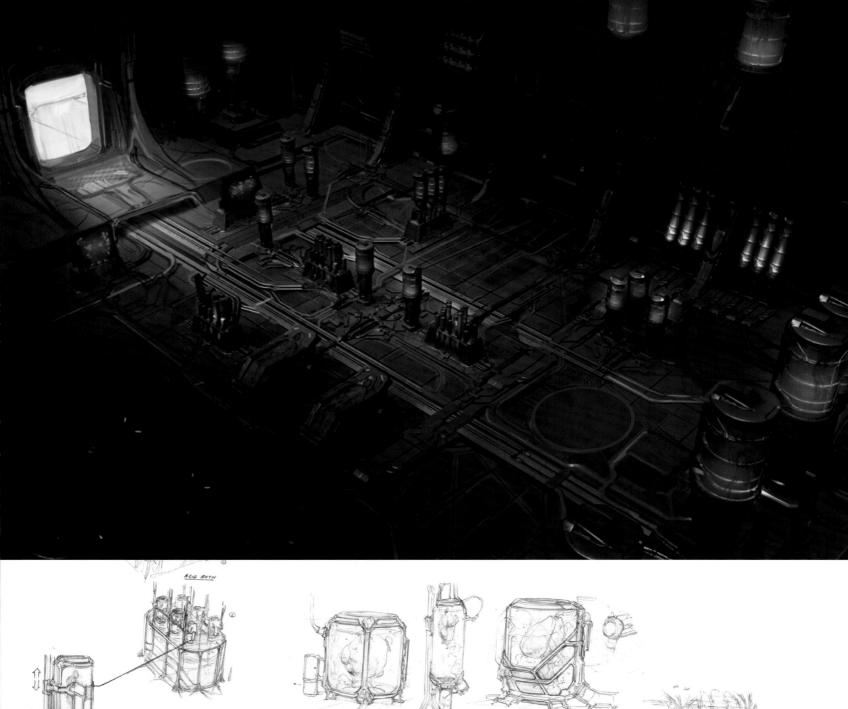

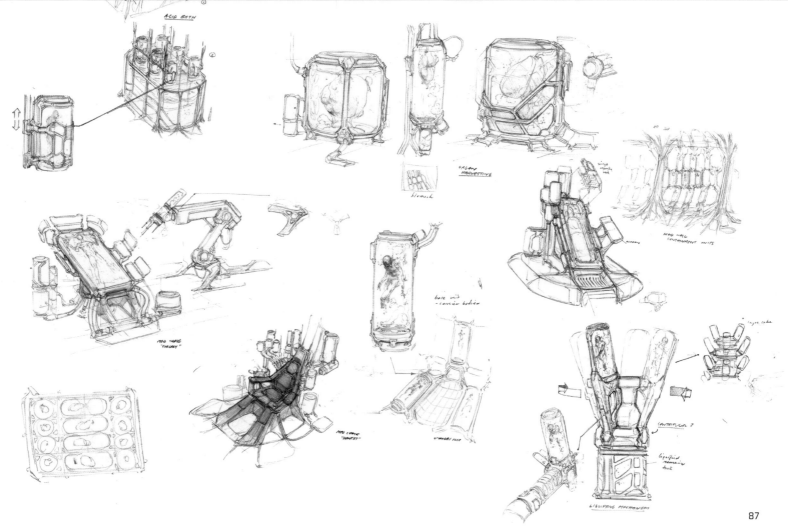

"It's always inspiring to see what the concept artists and animators are coming up with every day. You walk into each other's offices, and they show you something new, and you see the possibilities of the game before everyone else does. That can really energize you." —ZELJKO STRKAJ, LEAD TECHNICAL ARTIST

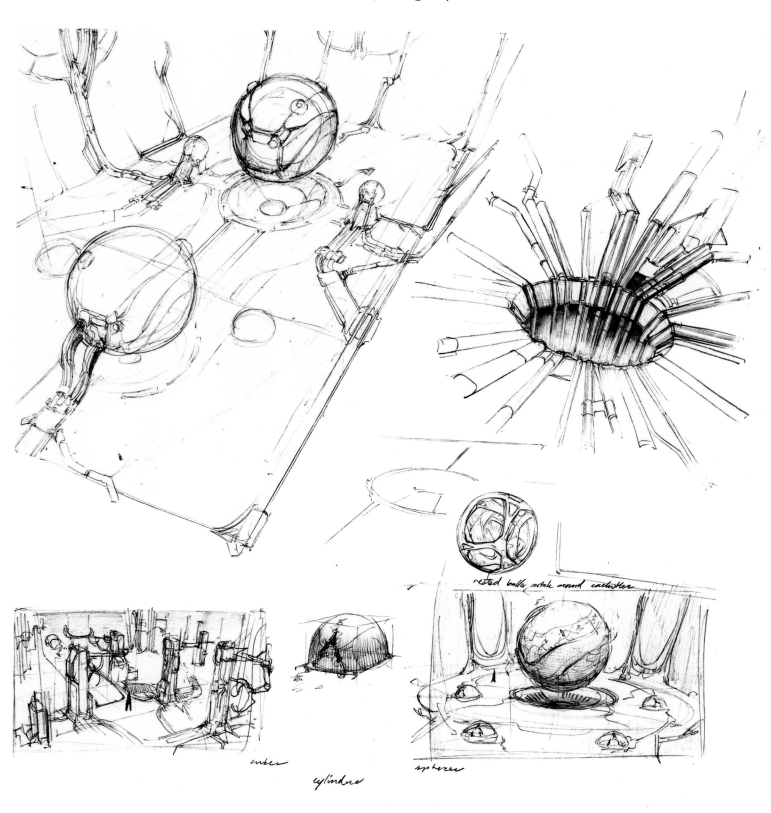

cubes

cylinders

nested balls rotate around each other

spheres

ABOVE: Rough sketches for alien technology and equipment. **OPPOSITE:** Concepts for an alien generator.

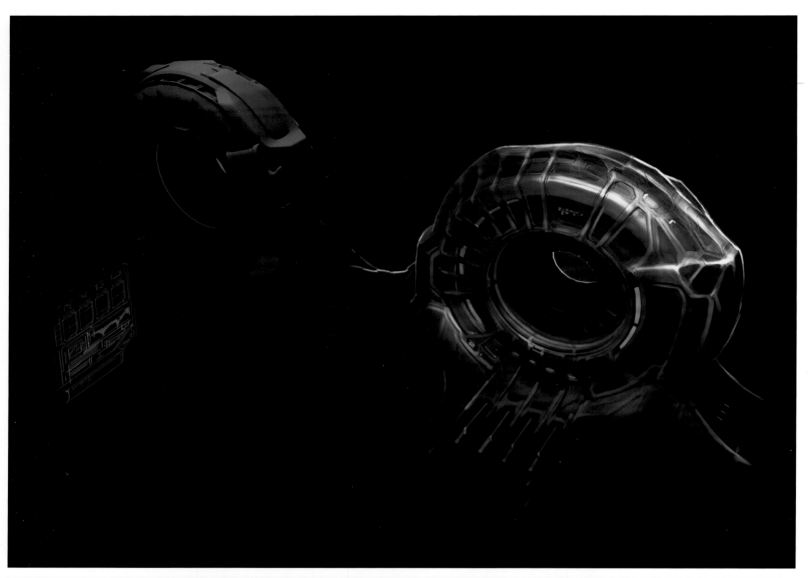

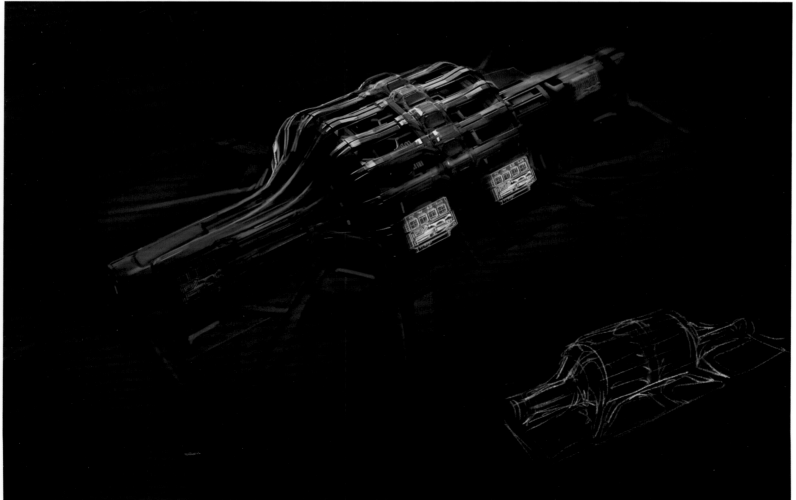

THE ALIENS

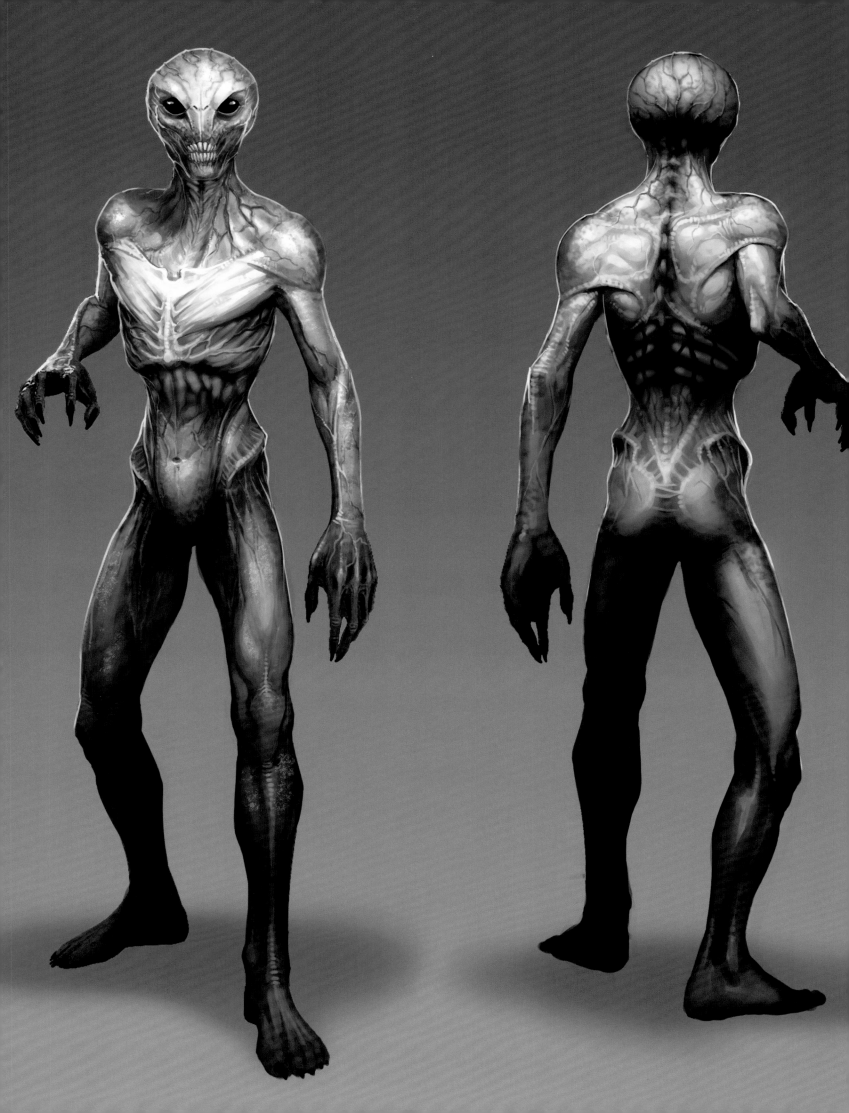

One of the first things game players may notice about *XCOM 2* is that the aliens are much more terrifying and powerful than before. "When you encounter aliens out in the field, your soldiers are not going to go toe-to-toe with them," says creative director Jake Solomon. "In the past twenty years, they've grown very strong. The important thing about the aliens is that soldiers are no longer a one-to-one match; there's no way to take on aliens without teamwork."

In this new world order, the aliens known as Sectoids have incorporated human DNA into their own. They're no longer a four-foot-tall species, standing about seven foot tall as they look at you with their beady, lizard-like eyes and flash their blindingly white teeth. But they still have that greyish-pink skin and eerie glow that emanates from their insides.

Also back for more dominance over humans are the apelike, heavy infantry Mutons, who have become stronger and now stand more upright. The terror unit aliens known as the Chryssalids—known for the way they make multiple clones of themselves—are also back in fine form. There's also Faceless, which has the ability to look like a civilian but wreaks havoc when he turns into an eight-foot-tall creature made of melting flesh. Humans also have to watch out for the heavy assault ADVENT robots known as Sectopods. And one of the most intriguing new alien invader species is the Vipers. A direct homage to the first *X-COM: UFO Defense* game, the sinister Vipers have been reverted to their original serpentine form in the new game.

"When we begin to conjure up these aliens, we always try to think of an animal they might resemble or remind us of," says lead animator Dennis Moellers. "For example, we thought about apes when we were animating the Mutons, although they are more intelligent and humanoid in this game. For something like the Berserker, we thought of a scarier version of the Hulk, with unpredictable movements and bigger-than-life reactions. To animate Faceless, we thought really hard about his transformation and the fact that it should hurt a lot to change, to have all those bones breaking and skin bubbling."

For concept artist Seamas Gallagher, the best way to come up with the appropriate designs is to go wild at first and then rein everything back to zero in on the perfect visuals. "In the case of the Faceless alien, for example, it sounded like a straightforward character on paper at first," he recalls. "But the design team had a very specific look in mind, so it took me a while to get it down. In the early iterations, he was much more lean and sinewy—but he was still muscular, with those waxy elements and bony contusions coming out of his body."

Since the game pays homage to all the cinematic alien invasion classics, there was an unwritten language about how to depict these characters' movements and interactions with the humans. As cinematics artist Andrew Currie notes, "We were able to take the camera away from the usual over-the-head view and bring it down to the surface level, so the player feels like they're witnessing the action as it happens to them. Many of our aliens are based on monsters familiar to fans from the horror genre. That's why we wanted to make the experience of dealing with these aliens as immersive as possible. It's not psychologically scary to look down on something. Here you can experience the battle with the aliens the way real soldiers would do in a battlefield."

PAGES 90–91: Artwork of a menacing Sectoid in a City Center. **LEFT:** Concepts for the Sectoid show how the aliens have grown thinner and taller than previous iterations.

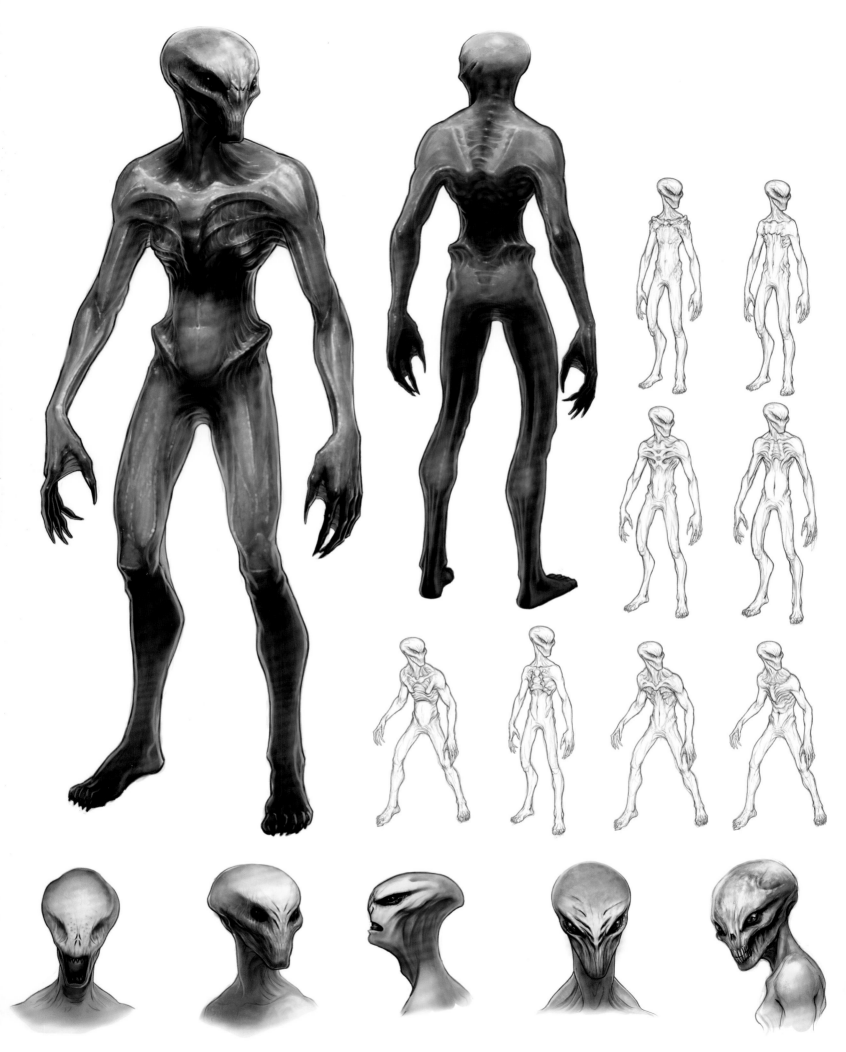

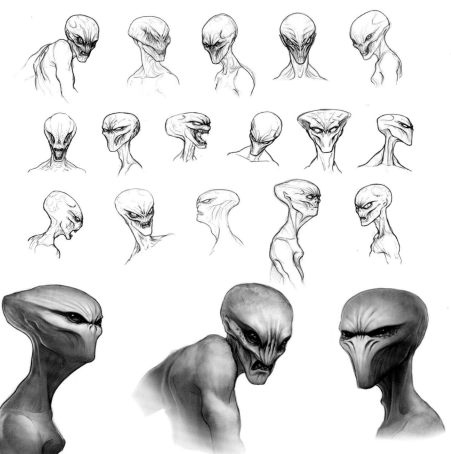

"We are looking at how things have developed in the past twenty years. Some of the aliens have evolved and don't look as brutish. We've updated the armors and changed the proportions a little bit. It's always easier to go wild at first and then rein things in if you need to." —SEAMAS GALLAGHER, CONCEPT ARTIST

OPPOSITE TOP: A concept for the evolved Sectoid blended with human genetics and chest variations. **LEFT:** Sectoid head designs. **TOP:** Early concept of the Sectoid head featuring a membrane covering over the mouth and eyes—aspects which have yet to completely evolve.

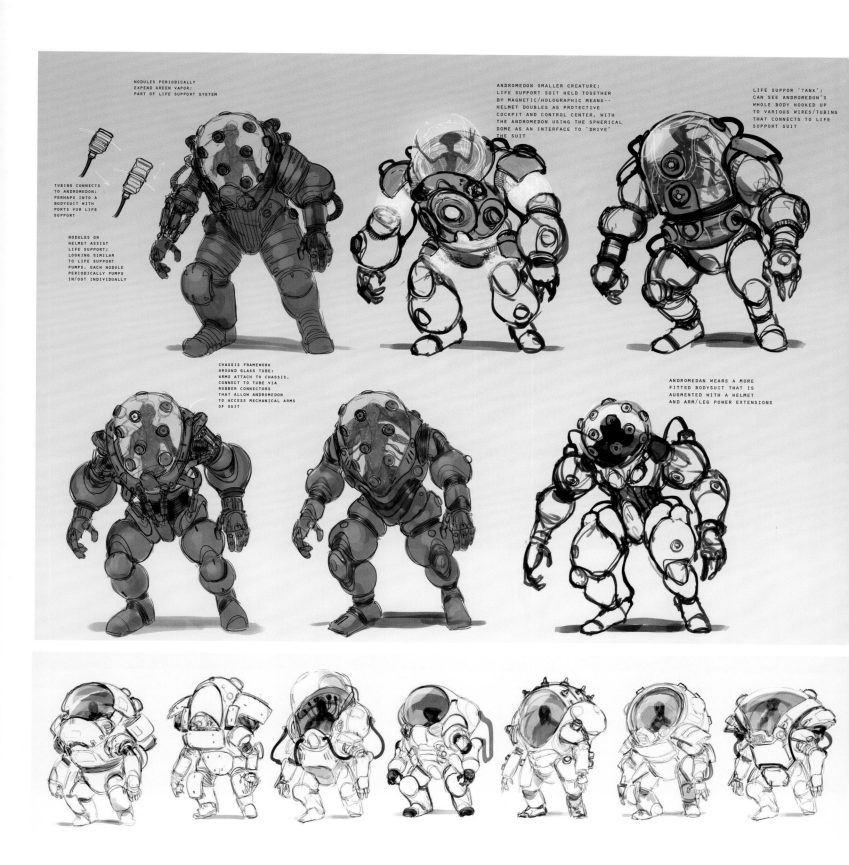

NODULES PERIODICALLY
EXPEND GREEN VAPOR;
PART OF LIFE SUPPORT SYSTEM

ANDROMEDON SMALLER CREATURE;
LIFE SUPPORT SUIT HELD TOGETHER
BY MAGNETIC/HOLOGRAPHIC MEANS--
HELMET DOUBLES AS PROTECTIVE
COCKPIT AND CONTROL CENTER, WITH
THE ANDROMEDON USING THE SPHERICAL
DOME AS AN INTERFACE TO 'DRIVE'
THE SUIT

LIFE SUPPOR 'TANK';
CAN SEE ANDROMEDON'S
WHOLE BODY HOOKED UP
TO VARIOUS WIRES/TUBING
THAT CONNECTS TO LIFE
SUPPORT SUIT

TUBING CONNECTS
TO ANDROMEDON;
PERHAPS INTO A
BODYSUIT WITH
PORTS FOR LIFE
SUPPORT

NODULES ON
HELMET ASSIST
LIFE SUPPORT;
LOOKING SIMILAR
TO LIFE SUPPORT
PUMPS. EACH NODULE
PERIODICALLY PUMPS
IN/OUT INDIVIDUALLY

CHASSIS FRAMEWORK
AROUND GLASS TUBE;
ARMS ATTACH TO CHASSIS,
CONNECT TO TUBE VIA
RUBBER CONNECTORS
THAT ALLOW ANDROMEDON
TO ACCESS MECHANICAL ARMS
OF SUIT

ANDROMEDAN WEARS A MORE
FITTED BODYSUIT THAT IS
AUGMENTED WITH A HELMET
AND ARM/LEG POWER EXTENSIONS

TOP: Rough concepts for the Andromedon show
the evolution of the alien housing. **ABOVE:** A series
of Andromedon rough mass sketches. **OPPOSITE
TOP:** The final Andromedon concept features a
respirator on its back that vents toxic gas.
OPPOSITE BOTTOM: A concept for a destroyed
Andromedon shows the unit in resurrected robot
mode, venting toxic gas, and leaking fluids.

TEARS IN TUBING
LEAK VAPOR OR
PUMP OUT SPURTS
OF GREEN LIQUID

DOME CAVITY BLASTED OPEN;
NOXIOUS GREEN VAPOR ISSUES
FORTH

HOSES/WIRING HANG
LIMPLY OUT OF CAVITY
LIKE ENTRAILS

VARIOUS PORTS IN
SUIT SPEW FORTH
VAPOR INTERMITANTLY

ARCHON ACTION SKETCHES

MAGNETIC/ANTI
GRAVITY PROPULSION
MECHANISM

OPPOSITE TOP: Animation concept sheet for Archon abilities. OPPOSITE BOTTOM: Two Archon concept variations; on the left, the team explored a version that featured a magnetic propulsion system. ABOVE: The final Archon concept, complete with the small jets used by the unit to achieve propulsion.

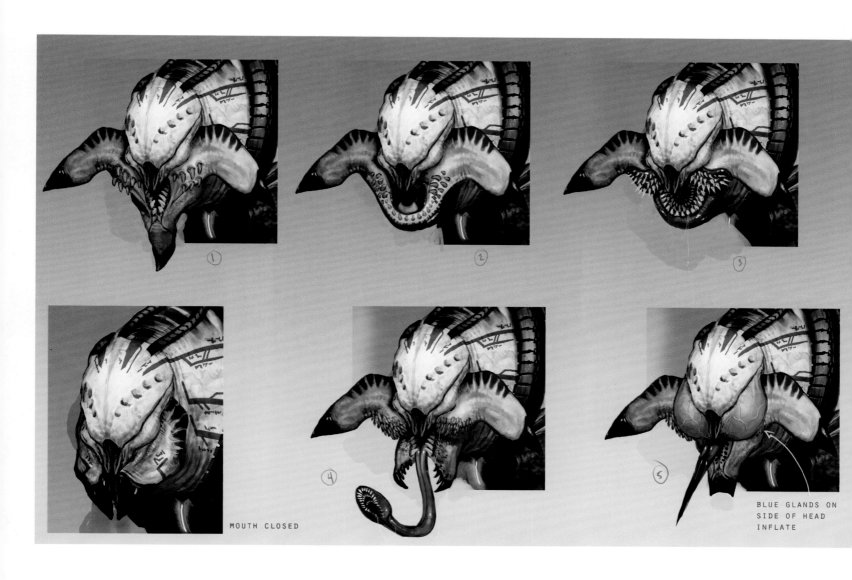

MOUTH CLOSED

BLUE GLANDS ON
SIDE OF HEAD
INFLATE

"When we begin our design process, especially for the aliens, we try to think of animals or characters they might resemble, for example, the Berserker alien is more like an ape or The Hulk." —DENNIS MOELLERS, LEAD ANIMATOR

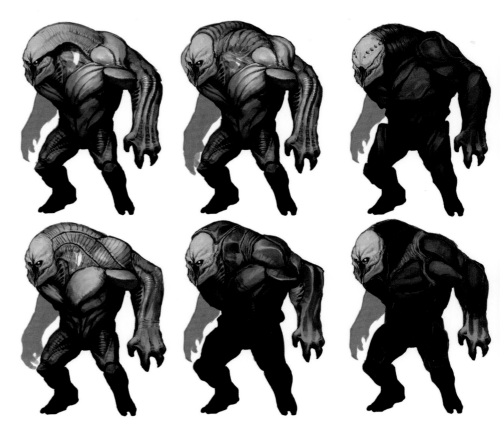

TOP: Berserker head and mouth concepts explore articulation of the jaws. RIGHT: Rough concepts for the Berserker used to refine the unit's musculature and organic armor plating. OPPOSITE: The Berserker rendered in-game model.

③

②

OPPOSITE: The Chryssalid rendered in-game model.
TOP: Chryssalid head concepts explored outer coloring, mouth articulation, and the feel of the eyes. ABOVE: Chryssalid rough concepts.

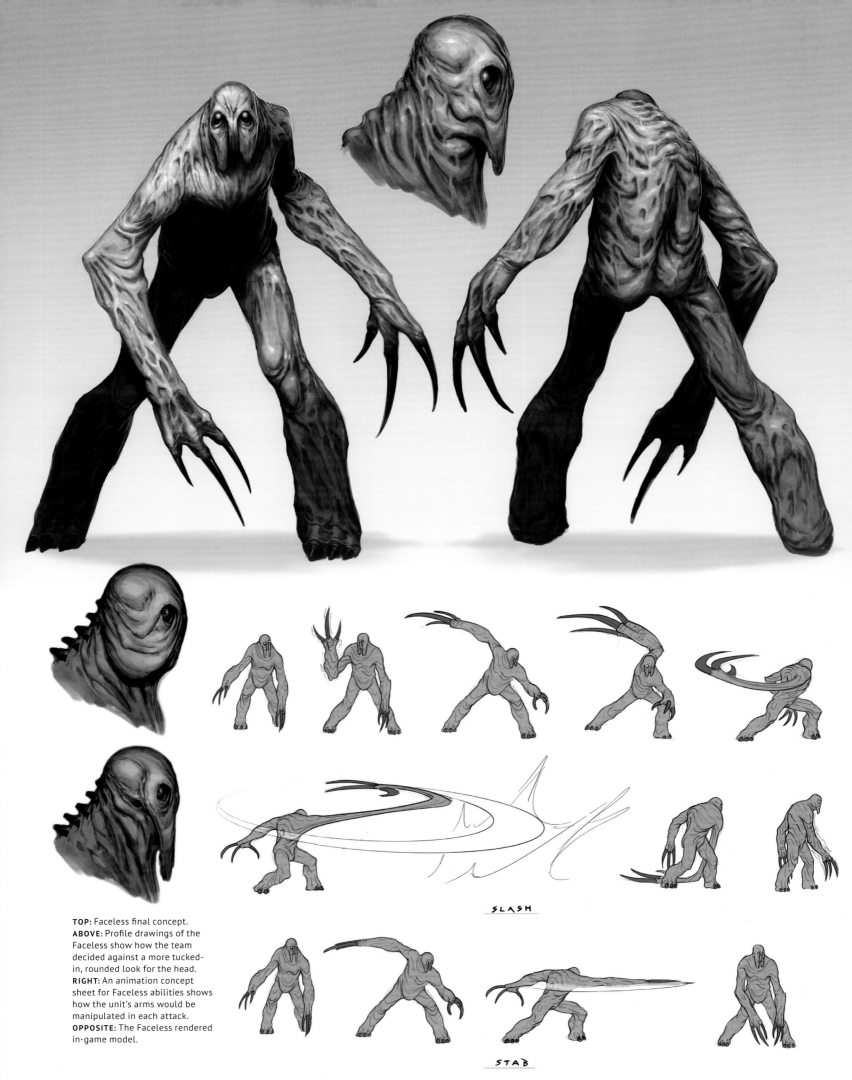

TOP: Faceless final concept.
ABOVE: Profile drawings of the Faceless show how the team decided against a more tucked-in, rounded look for the head.
RIGHT: An animation concept sheet for Faceless abilities shows how the unit's arms would be manipulated in each attack.
OPPOSITE: The Faceless rendered in-game model.

SLASH

STAB

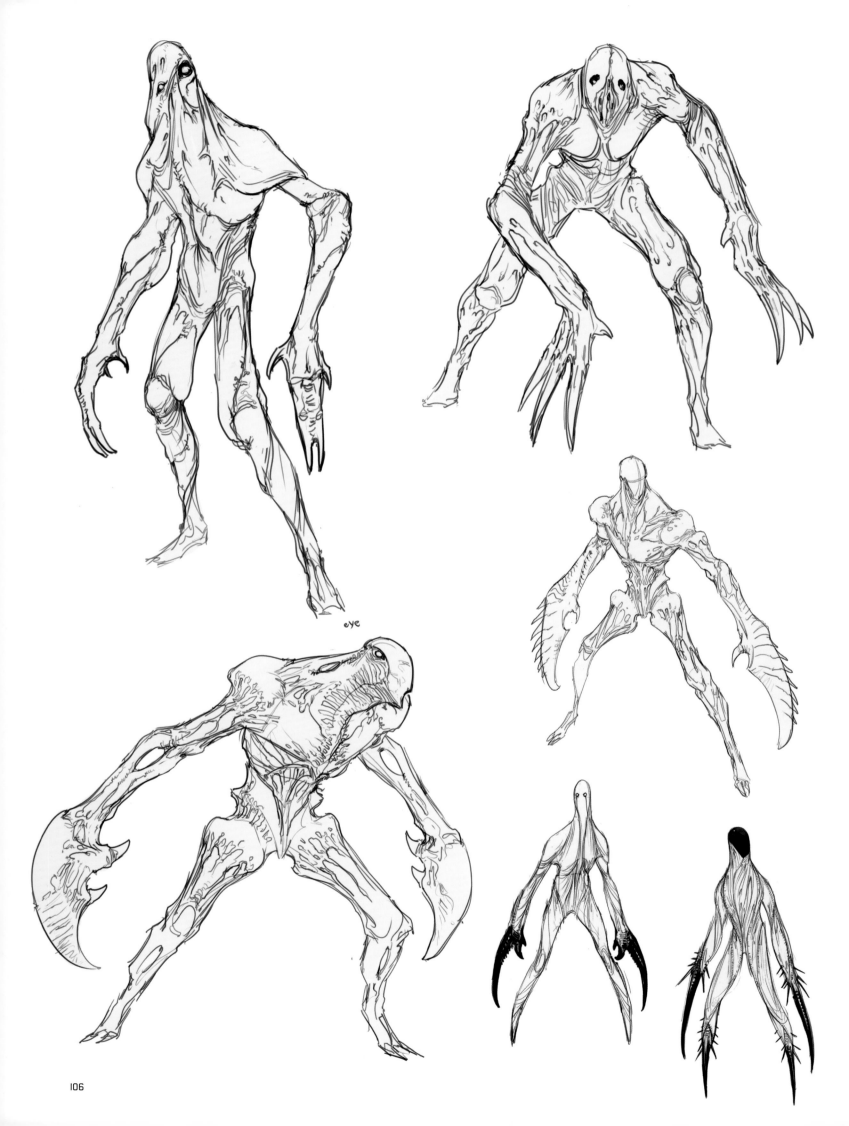

eye

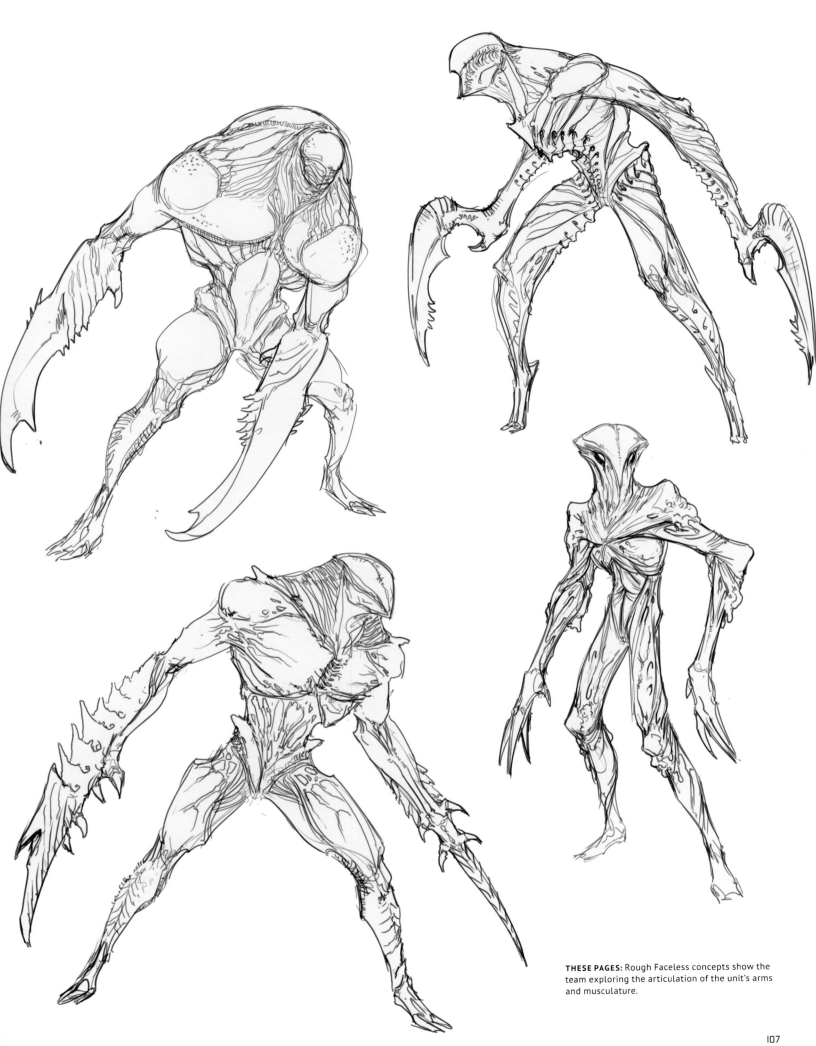

THESE PAGES: Rough Faceless concepts show the team exploring the articulation of the unit's arms and musculature.

THIS PAGE: Rough concepts of the Gatekeeper in its open state explore the organic elements inside this alien.
OPPOSITE TOP LEFT: Explorations of the closed state. The bottom sphere is the final closed state concept.
OPPOSITE TOP RIGHT: The final open state concept.
OPPOSITE BOTTOM: Rough concepts of the Gatekeeper in its open state.

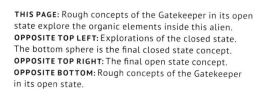

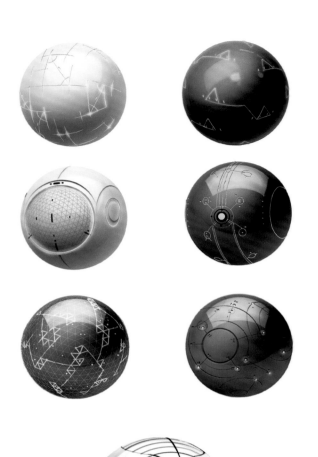

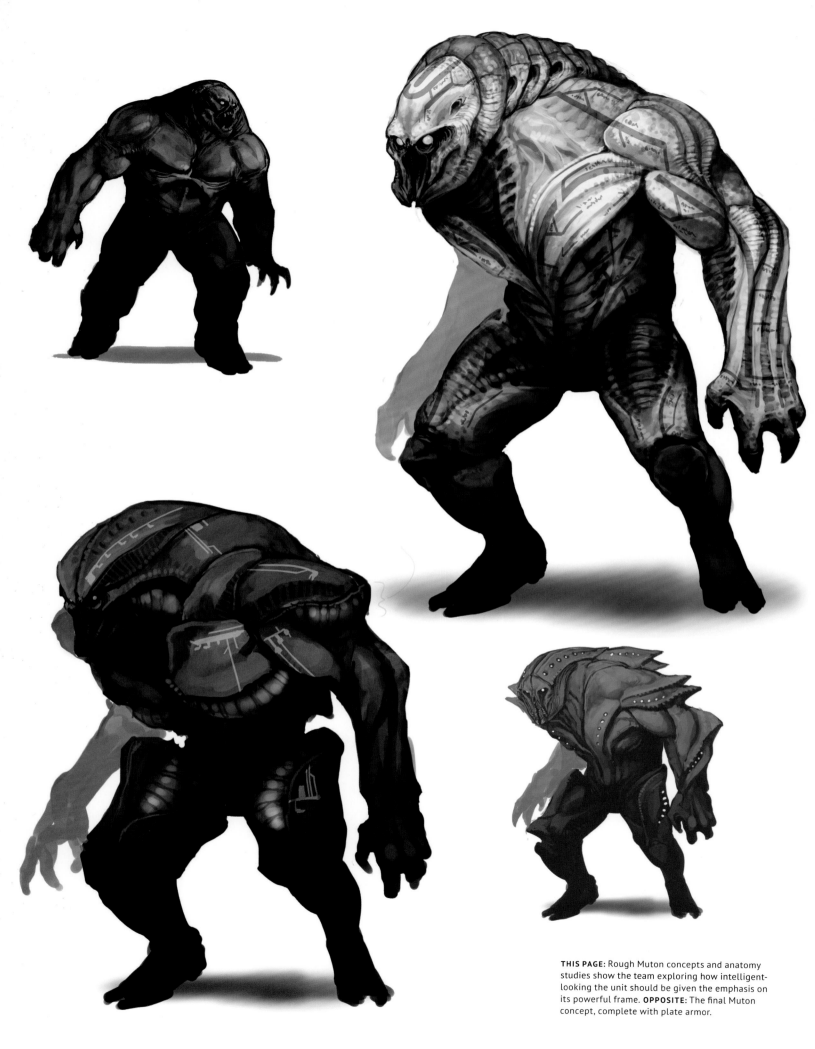

THIS PAGE: Rough Muton concepts and anatomy studies show the team exploring how intelligent-looking the unit should be given the emphasis on its powerful frame. OPPOSITE: The final Muton concept, complete with plate armor.

THESE PAGES: Rough Muton concepts exploring
a more formfitting and integrated armor.

OPPOSITE TOP: Rough Viper concepts included ventral spines that were removed from later iterations. OPPOSITE BOTTOM: Animation concept sheet for the Viper's Bind and Pull abilities. RIGHT: The final Viper concept, complete with armored exoskeleton.

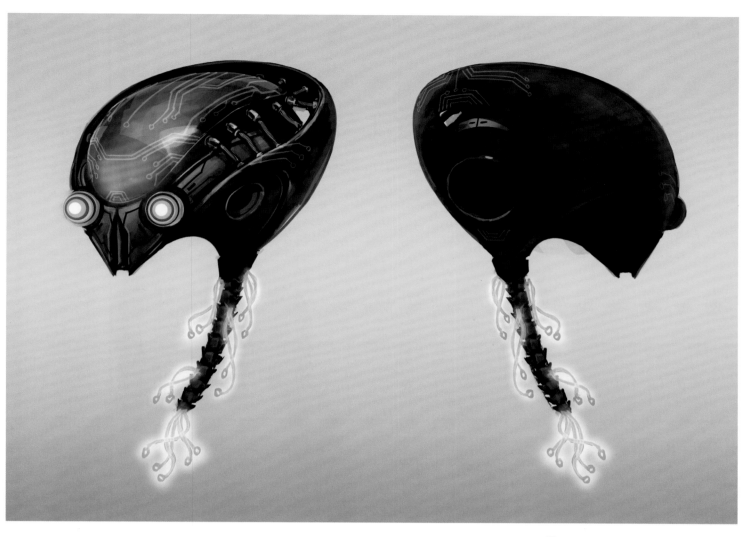

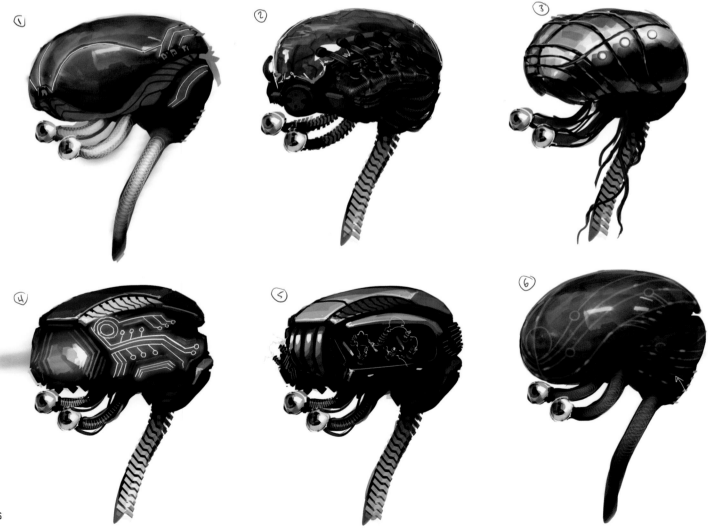

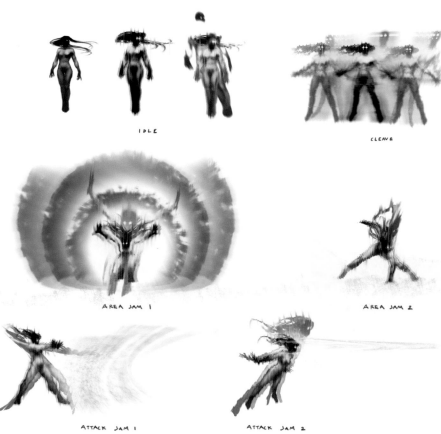

IDLE

CLEAVE

WALL

AREA JAM 1

AREA JAM 2

ATTACK JAM 1

ATTACK JAM 2

OPPOSITE TOP: The final Codex brain concept shows an intermingling of robotic and organic elements. **OPPOSITE BOTTOM:** Codex brain studies explore a variety of colors far brighter than the final design. **TOP:** The final Codex concept. **ABOVE:** An animation concept sheet exploring a variety of Codex abilities.

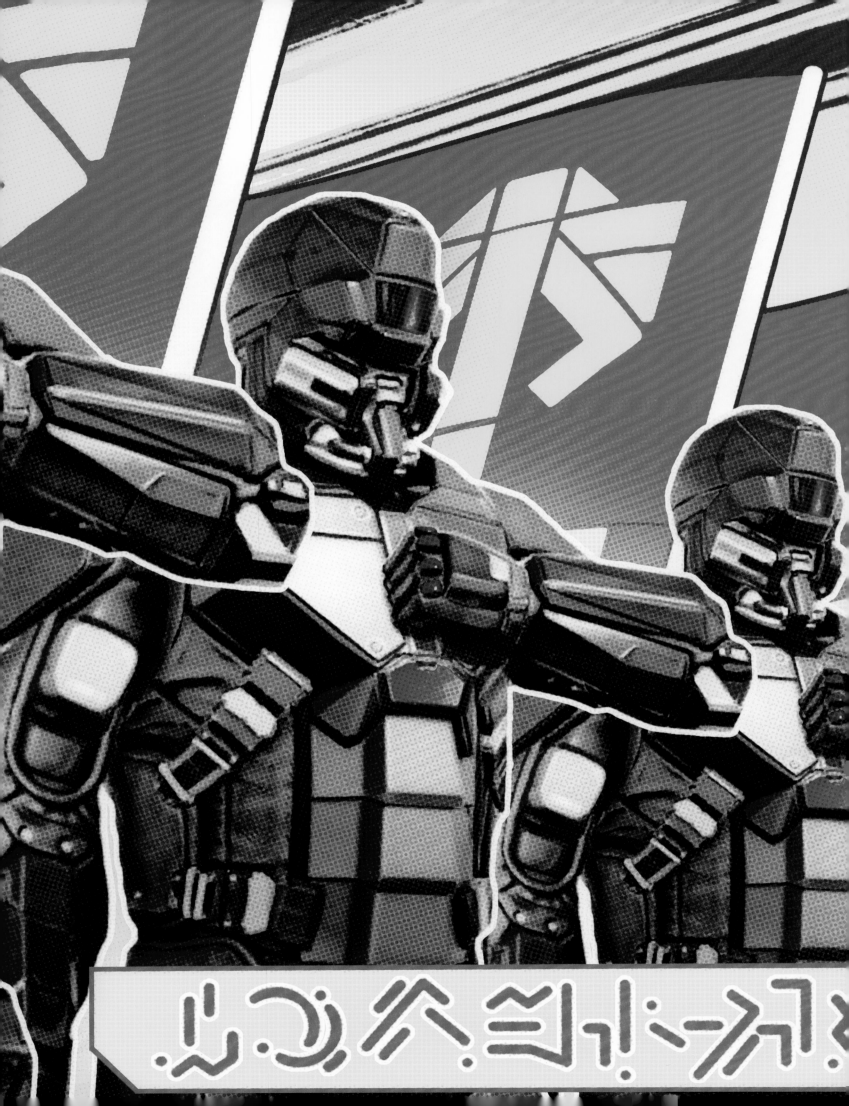

CHAPTER 4

THE ADVENT

The ADVENT are the aliens' direct hand in controlling Earth. They administer the eerily clean cities and gene clinics, endlessly extolling how "the Elders" are uplifting humanity. And their armored troops are the mailed fist that keeps order.

Visually, the ADVENT are a striking change from the rough, irregular forces of XCOM at the start of the game. Their visual identity is made up of hard, angular shapes in primal blacks, whites, and reds. As senior concept artist Aaron Yamada-Hanff explains, "The ADVENT came from a stealthy, military hardware visual identity, with complex hard geometry, in contrast with the simpler geometry of the city centers. As a basic design principle, having that contrast is necessary."

Like *XCOM's* soldiers, the ADVENT units are built as modular elements, with the different classes of soldiers sharing common design with enhancements that help identify their role. Shieldbearers have their enhanced armor. Officers have larger helmets and capes, and the Stun Lancer's melee weapon is slung over his back. This helps players identify which enemies they're facing at a glance when the battle unfolds.

Observing real-life soldiers helped the design team get solid inspiration for the designs. "You are constantly looking for references," says concept artist Seamas Gallagher. "You pick and choose from everything you can find. You throw them all in a bag and see what eventually comes out. You do fifty different iterations, and then you take five of them, and then something rises to the top. More often than not, you take elements from various iterations and then incorporate them into one final design. It's very rare that you hit it out of the park on that first attempt."

The ADVENT serves as the first antagonist and most common enemy in *XCOM 2*. During the course of the game, players discover the sinister truth behind the ADVENT's soldiers and their relationship to the aliens: The full-face helmets hide a humanity warped by the aliens in the same way that previously conquered species were transformed. Overcoming a corrupted enemy with every appearance of technical sophistication and hardware advantage is one of the great joys of *XCOM 2*.

PAGES 118–119: An ADVENT propaganda poster.
OPPOSITE: Final concept for an ADVENT MEC Mark II.

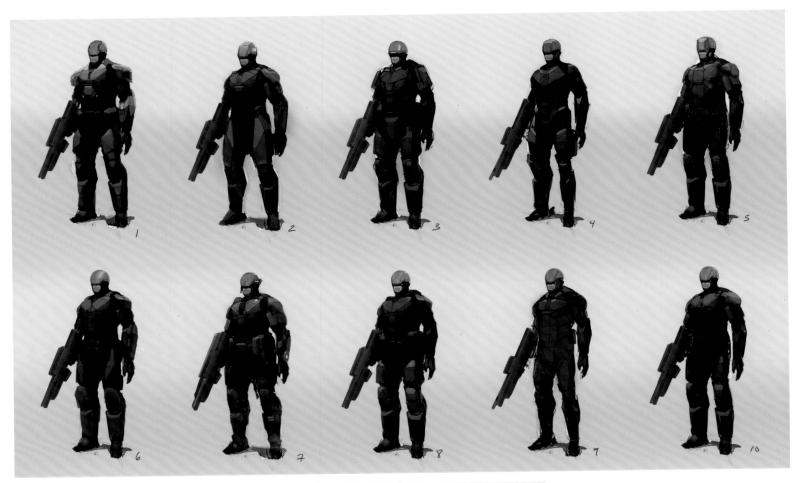

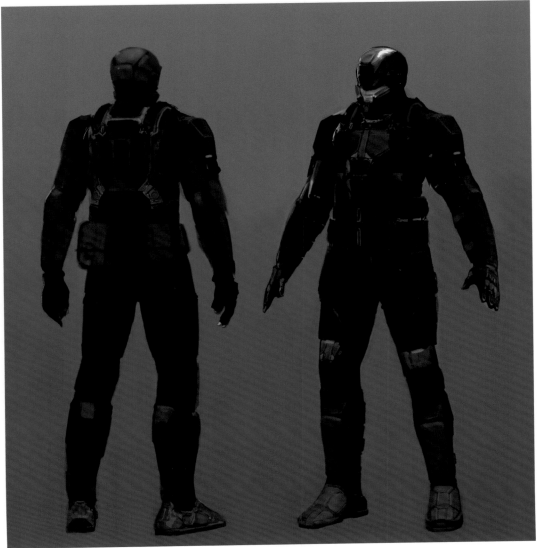

"*XCOM's* visual style is not realism—we get to dramatize and exaggerate things a little more and offer a heroic take on the action."

—DENNIS MOELLERS, LEAD ANIMATOR

OPPOSITE: An in-game render of the ADVENT Trooper. **TOP:** ADVENT Trooper silhouettes. **LEFT:** ADVENT Trooper final concept.

SHIELD BEARER

CAPTAIN

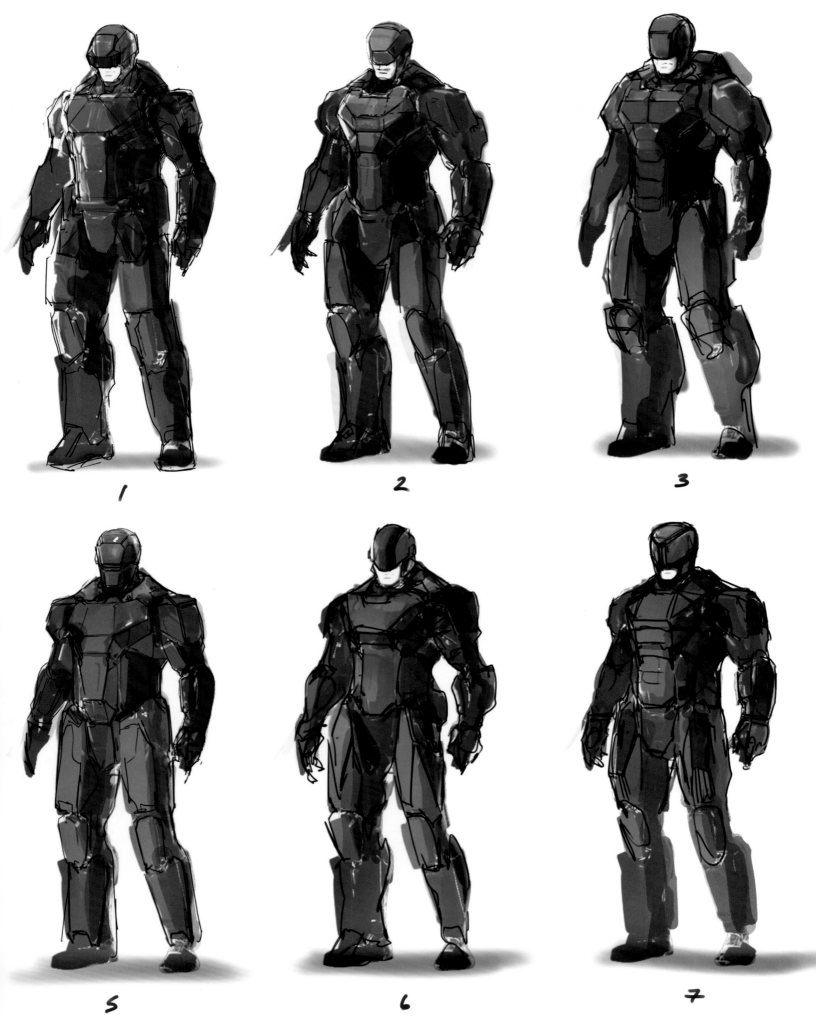

1

2

3

5

6

7

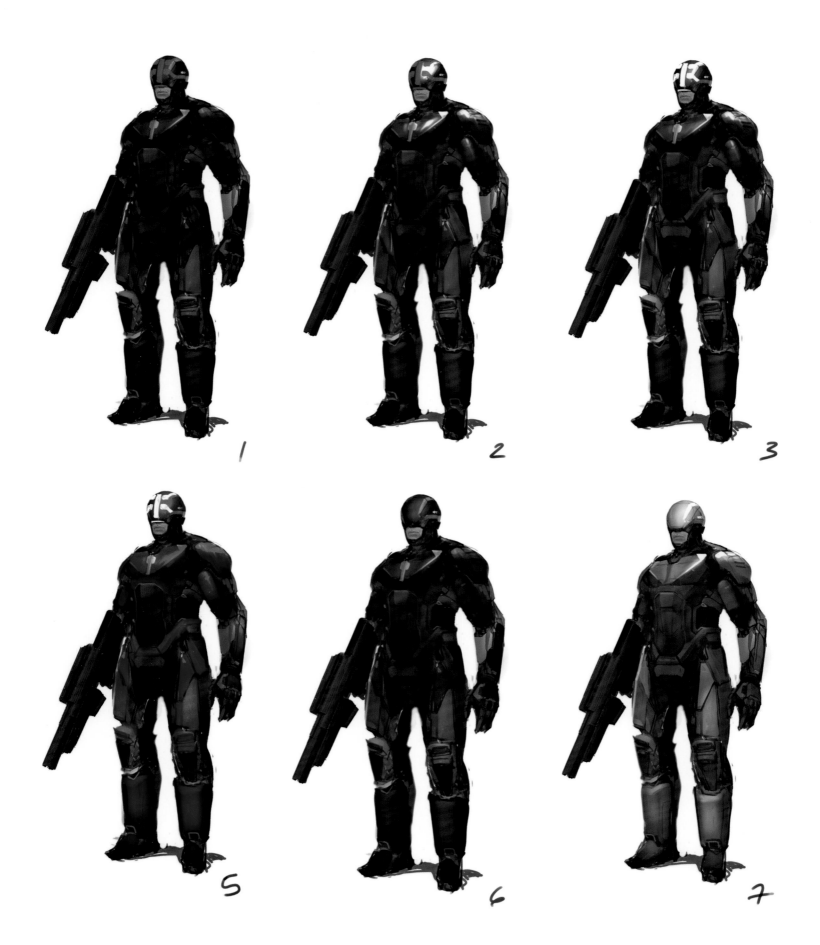

1

2

3

5

6

7

PREVIOUS PAGES: Concepts and rough sketches for the ADVENT Stun Lancer, Shieldbearer, and Captain. **ABOVE:** Color studies for the ADVENT Trooper. **OPPOSITE:** ADVENT Stunlancer helmet concept callout. **PAGES 128–129:** Artwork showing an ADVENT Trooper engaging an enemy.

 ADVENT RECRUITMENT CENTER

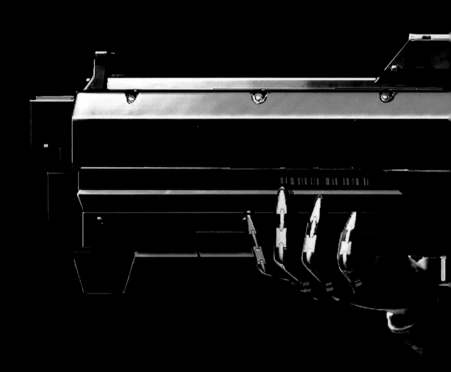

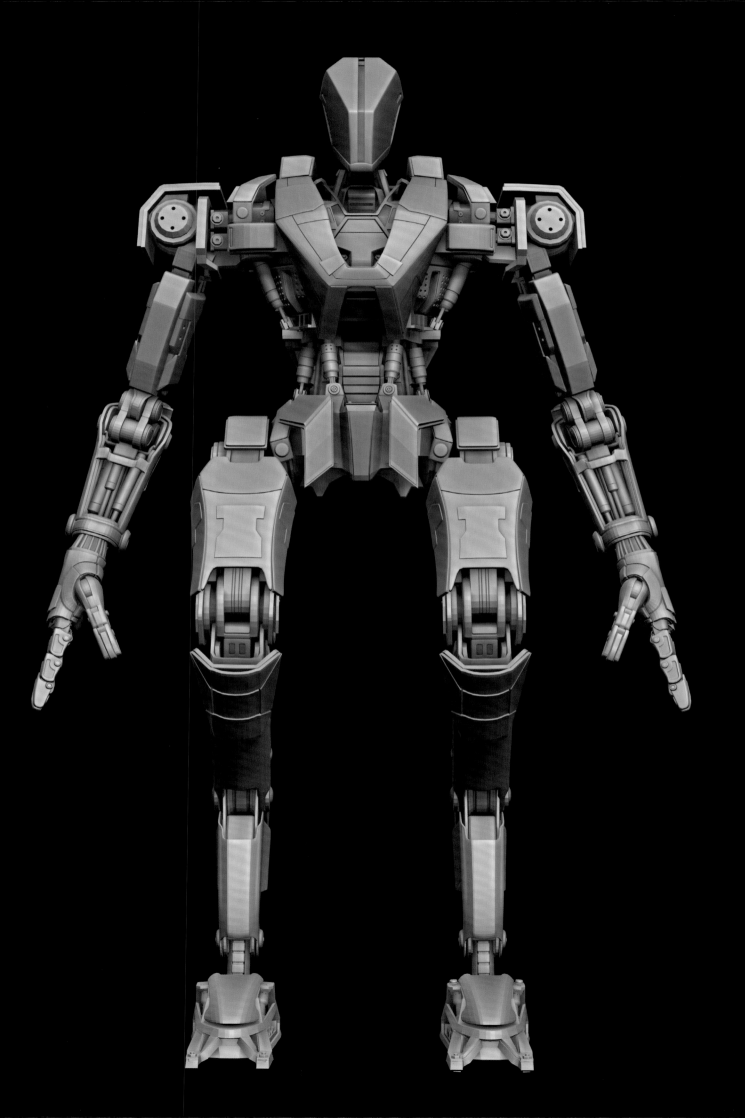

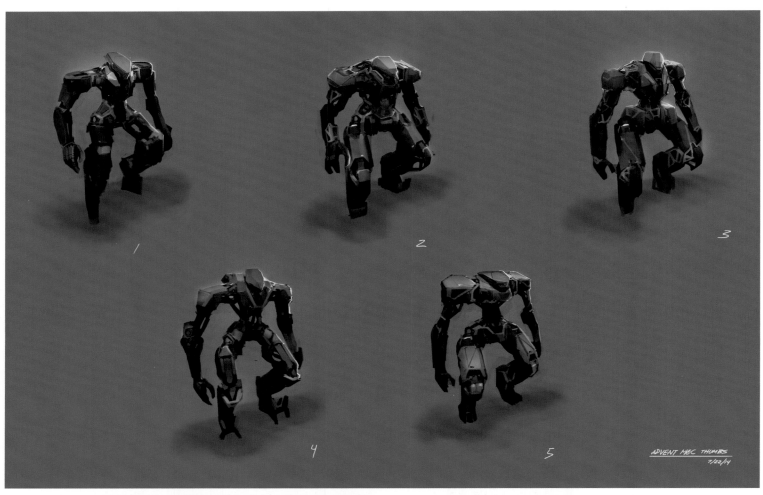

OPPOSITE: An ADVENT MEC high-resolution render. **THIS PAGE:** ADVENT MEC concepts and color exploration.

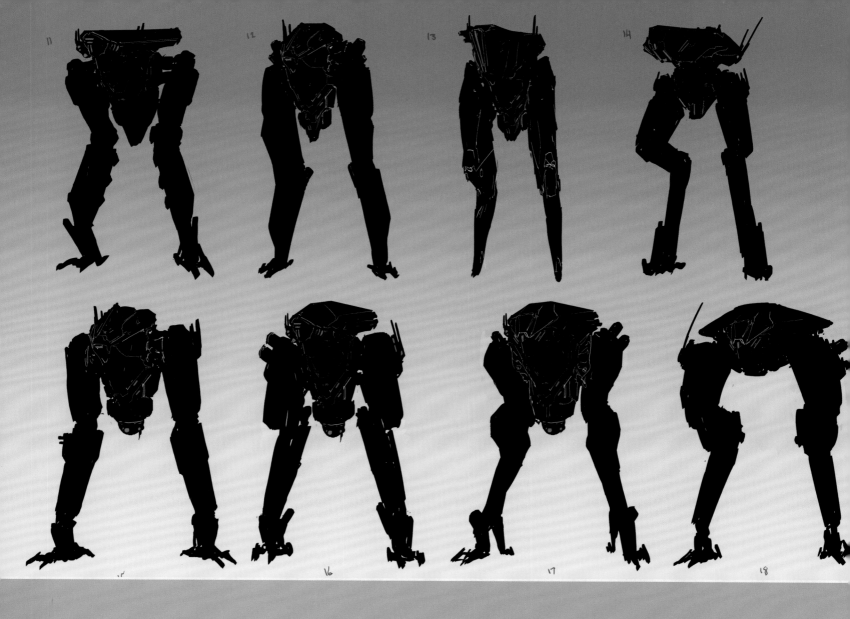

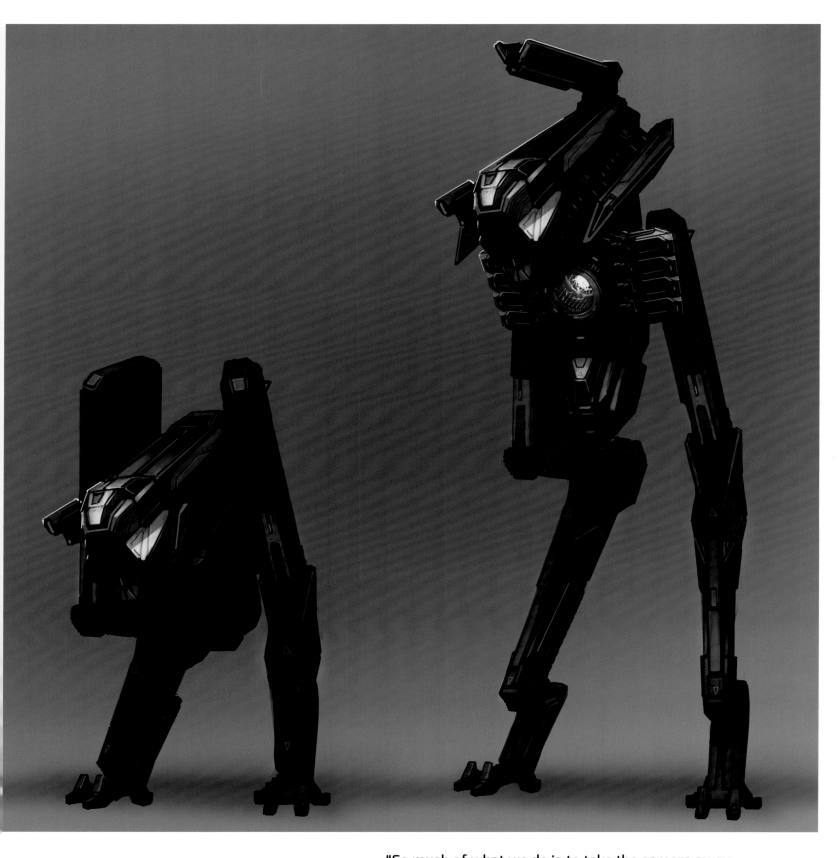

"So much of what we do is to take the camera away from over-the-head strategy view and bring it down as if you're witnessing the action. Many of our aliens are based on monsters seen in horror genre—and it's not very scary psychologically to look down on something, so our goal is to allow the player to experience the battle the way the soldiers do." —ANDREW CURRIE, CINEMATICS

OPPOSITE: Mass drawings and rough concepts for the ADVENT Sectopod. THIS PAGE: The final ADVENT Sectopod concept, including designs for the unit's extended two-story-high transformation.

ABOVE: Rough ADVENT Troop Transport concepts and mass drawings. **OPPOSITE:** The final concept for the ADVENT Troop Transport vehicle.

LANDED

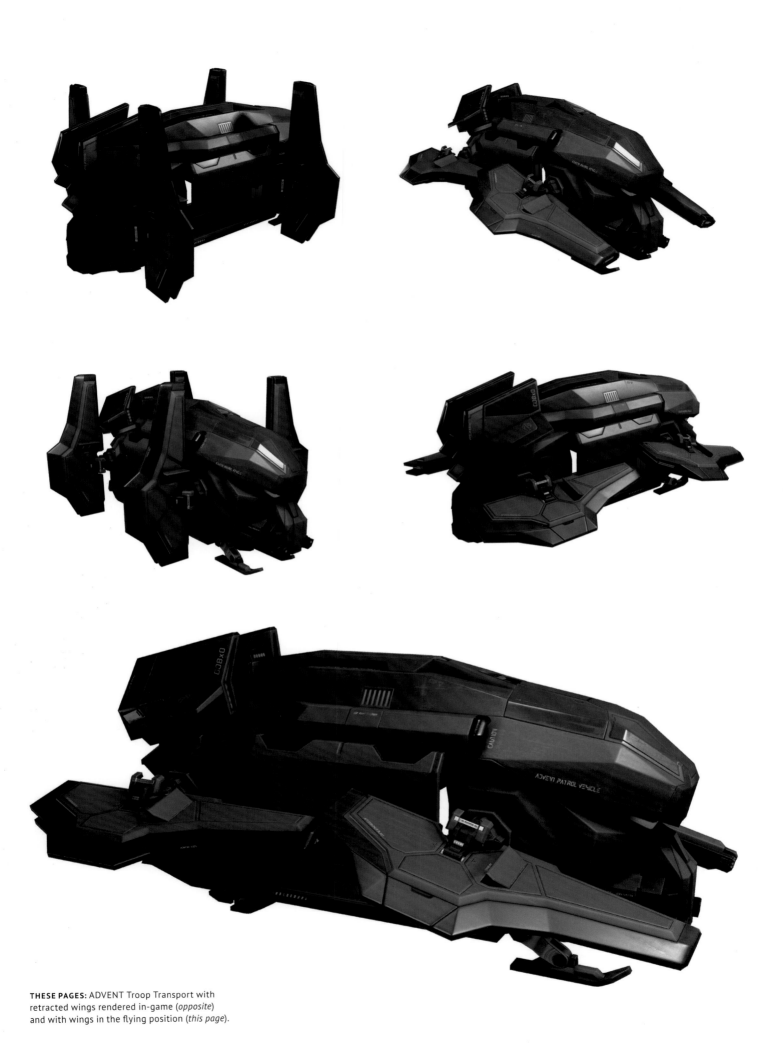

THESE PAGES: ADVENT Troop Transport with
retracted wings rendered in-game (*opposite*)
and with wings in the flying position (*this page*).

SLIDING SIDE DOOR

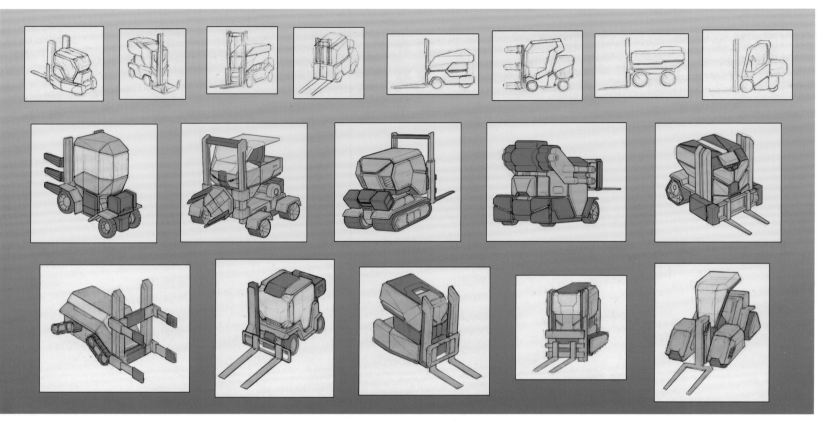

OPPOSITE TOP: Several ADVENT Train and boxcar concepts. **OPPOSITE BOTTOM:** Concept for the ADVENT Prisoner Transport Van. **TOP:** Rough ADVENT Forklift concepts show how the team began with more conventional designs. **ABOVE:** The final ADVENT Forklift concept.

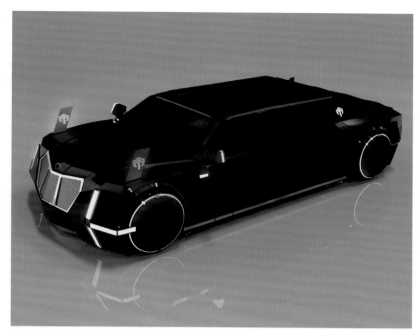

STATIONARY PIECE: WHEEL
GAURD FITS OVER FRONT WHEELS

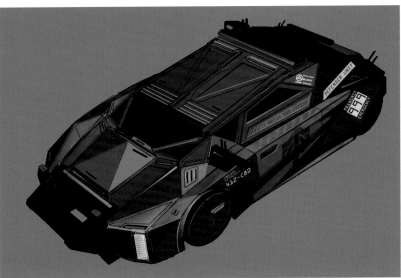

OPPOSITE: ADVENT VIP Car concepts show chrome accents and holographic flags on the hood.
TOP: ADVENT Rapid Response Car final concept.
ABOVE: Earlier ADVENT Rapid Response Car rough concepts included more red in their designs.

XCOM

CHAPTER 5

ORIGINAL "PRISTI
CONVENTIONAL A

In a world that has surrendered to alien invaders, the remnant XCOM forces have reconvened to expose the sinister truth behind the invasion and defeat the alien threat. While the game's experienced XCOM soldiers echo the ones players last saw in *Enemy Unknown*, they also have their own distinct look and characteristics.

The Sharpshooter specializes in using a sniper rifle as a primary weapon, while the Ranger is an evolved version of the Assault class who specializes in close combat with shotguns but also is equipped with the game's first machete-like blade weapon. The Grenadier is able to cause damage to alien forces by blowing things up, while the Specialist uses a very cool-looking drone called a Gremlin to surprise enemies, support allies, and zero in on long-range hacking jobs.

One of the aspects of the game that has created a huge, positive fan response is the way that players have much more control over their soldier's appearance. In this new installment of the *XCOM* series, you can swap genders and ethnicities, as well as play with the look of the arms, torso, pants, headgear, and hairstyles. "We have some really cool-looking soldiers," says creative director Jake Solomon. "They can have big beards; they can have really awesome haircuts; they can have some cool stuff that gives them a lot of character and fits the idea that they're this sort of hardened group. They're not fresh-out-of-the-barracks Johnny Soldier; this is really more of a *Sons of Anarchy*–type of squad."

Solomon advises gamers to wait until the soldiers have survived some challenges before they begin customizing them, especially since more interesting options will be available later in the game. "We try to make it easy for the player to customize, but you can spend a lot more time customizing your soldiers, which you should not do unless you have relative certainty that you're either going to reload them when they die or that they are going to survive," he says. "So, don't do that on rookies because you'll have wasted a lot of time."

Lead character modeler Chris Sulzbach says one of the most interesting aspects of his job was working closely with the animators to develop a distinct visual language for the various types of soldiers. "We wanted the silhouettes to convey immediately what kind of armor the soldiers are wearing," he explains. "We removed class base from the game in favor of more customization options, since we discovered earlier on that more customization was what the community wanted to see. Since *XCOM 2* is a game about people dying, there's a permanent sense of death, which can be a double-edged sword. You can spend all this time customizing a character, and it becomes more painful when you lose them. So you start out with these rookie characters and once they get to a certain rank, you get the honor of customizing them—at that point, we reward the players who waited by unlocking more veteran customization. You unlock tattoo options, different haircuts, different head crops, and baseline customizations."

Of course, it helps the process greatly when the artists act out the game in front of a mirror and take good notes. "You'd be surprised how much of the characters actually come from the animators acting out with some video references," says lead animator Dennis Moellers. "You can hear the animators acting out various scenarios as you walk through the hallways of the studio. For example, one of our animators, Justin Thomas, actually tapes cardboard pieces to himself to really get into character. They exaggerate the movements in the animation, and it really helps bring things to life."

PAGES 142–143: The iconic symbol of XCOM in hologram. **OPPOSITE:** An exploration of XCOM soldiers as a guerrilla force.

"We developed a clean visual language for the different types of soldiers we have in the game. The silhouettes convey immediately what kind of armor they're wearing. The class base is a bit different because we removed that in favor of more customization options. You are able to do colors, patterns, change out arms, torsos, legs, helmets, etc. Basically, you can make your Rangers look like whatever you want them to look like."

—CHRIS SULZBACH, CHARACTER LEAD

OPPOSITE TOP AND ABOVE: Central Officer Bradford, twenty years after the invasion. Grizzled and aged, he has changed a great deal, as seen in both full body and head concepts. **BELOW:** Studies exploring Central Officer Bradford's costuming.

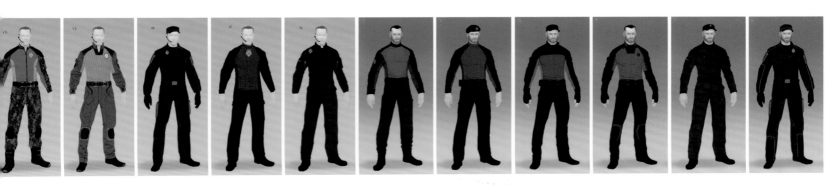

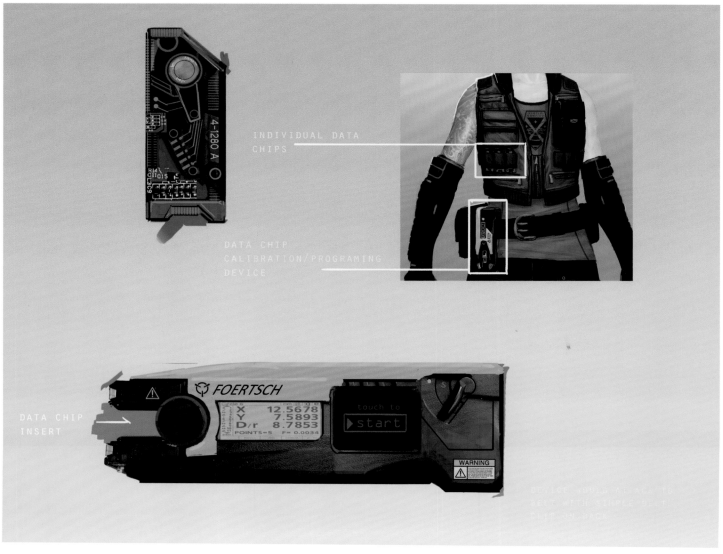

INDIVIDUAL DATA
CHIPS

DATA CHIP
CALIBRATION/PROGRAMING
DEVICE

DATA CHIP
INSERT

FOERTSCH

X   12.5678
Y   7.5893
D/r 8.7853
POINTS=5   F= 0.0034

touch to
▶start

WARNING

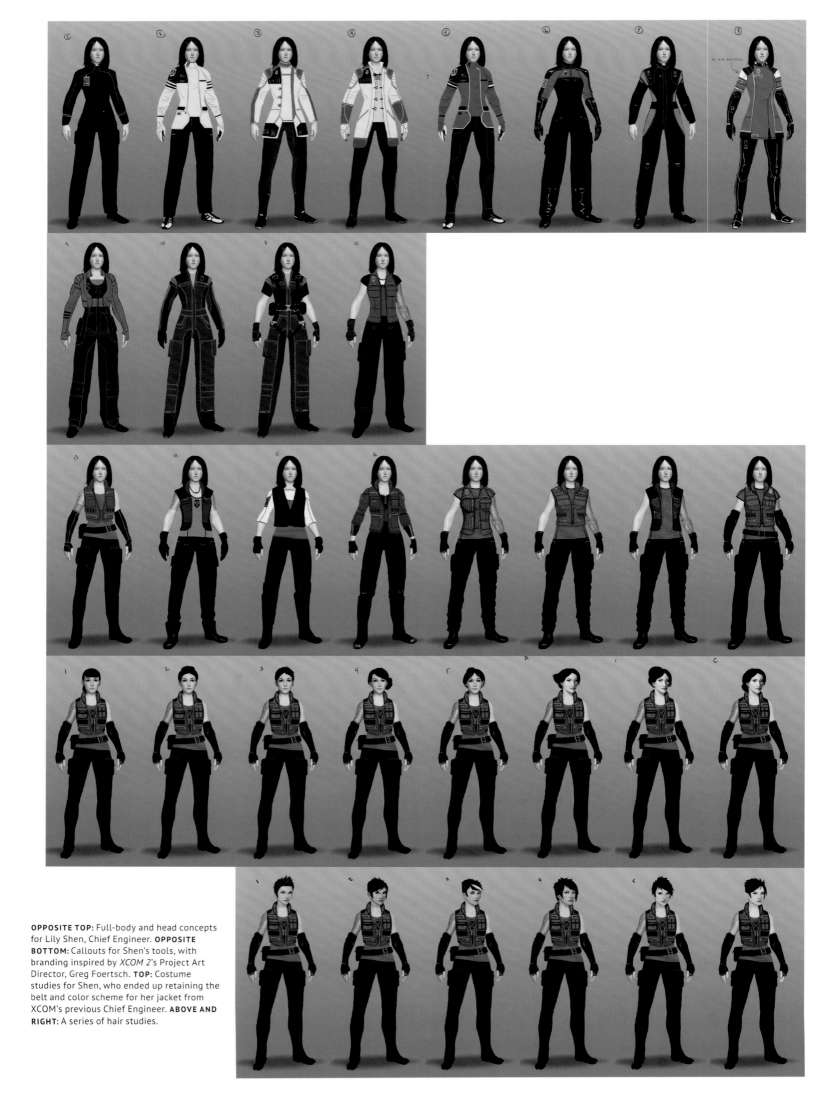

OPPOSITE TOP: Full-body and head concepts for Lily Shen, Chief Engineer. **OPPOSITE BOTTOM:** Callouts for Shen's tools, with branding inspired by *XCOM 2*'s Project Art Director, Greg Foertsch. **TOP:** Costume studies for Shen, who ended up retaining the belt and color scheme for her jacket from XCOM's previous Chief Engineer. **ABOVE AND RIGHT:** A series of hair studies.

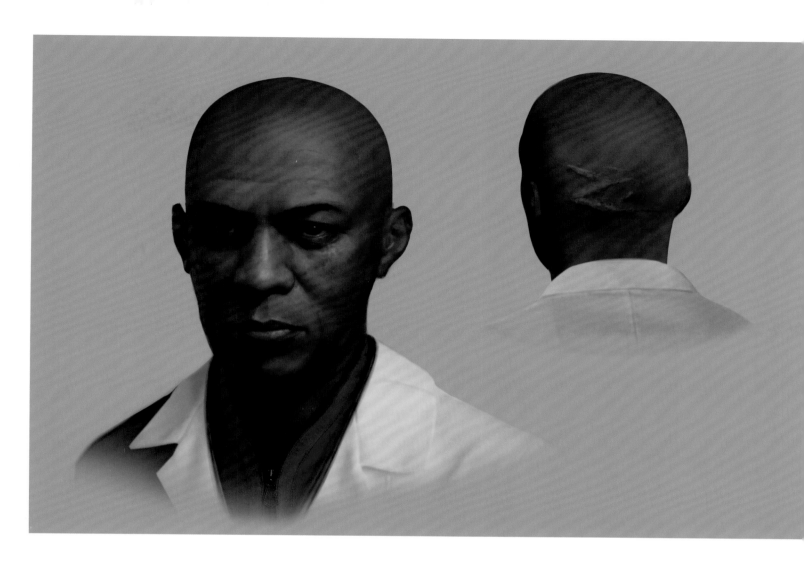

TOP AND RIGHT: Head concepts and studies for Dr. Tygan, Chief Scientist. The back of his head reveals a deep scar where his ADVENT chip implant was removed. **OPPOSITE TOP:** Costuming studies for Dr. Tygan. **OPPOSITE BOTTOM:** Final concept for Dr. Tygan. His clothing is clearly more influenced by the styles of the City Centers and his time prior to joining XCOM.

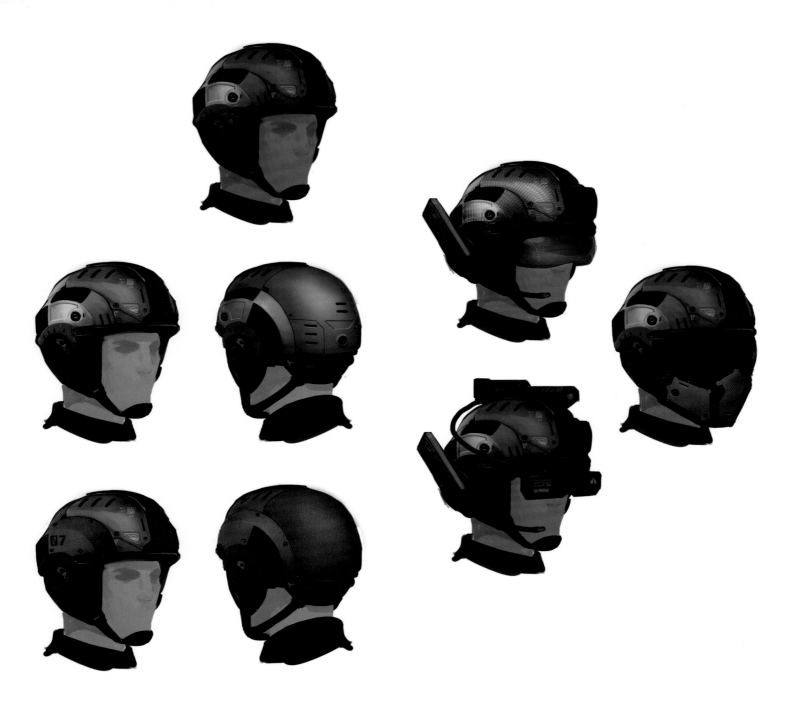

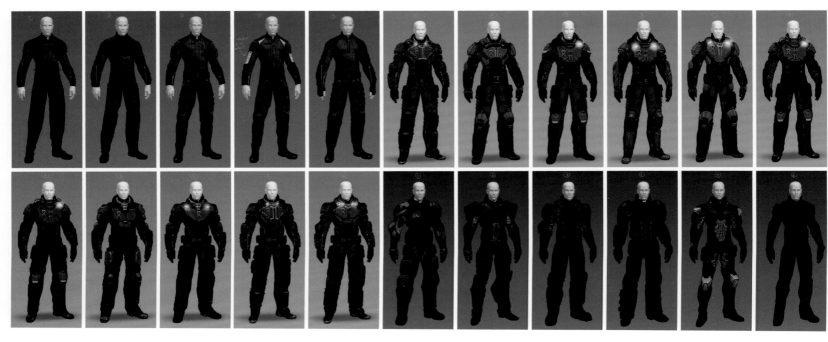

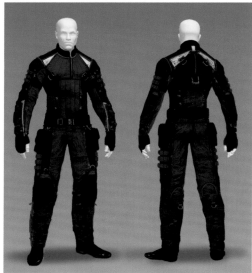

OPPOSITE TOP: Conventional helmet concepts were designed with modular parts. **OPPOSITE BOTTOM:** Underlay uniform and base line conventional armor studies. **LEFT:** A Ranger class conventional soldier, with the secondary weapon of a sword. **TOP AND ABOVE:** Final baseline conventional armor and underlay uniform concepts.

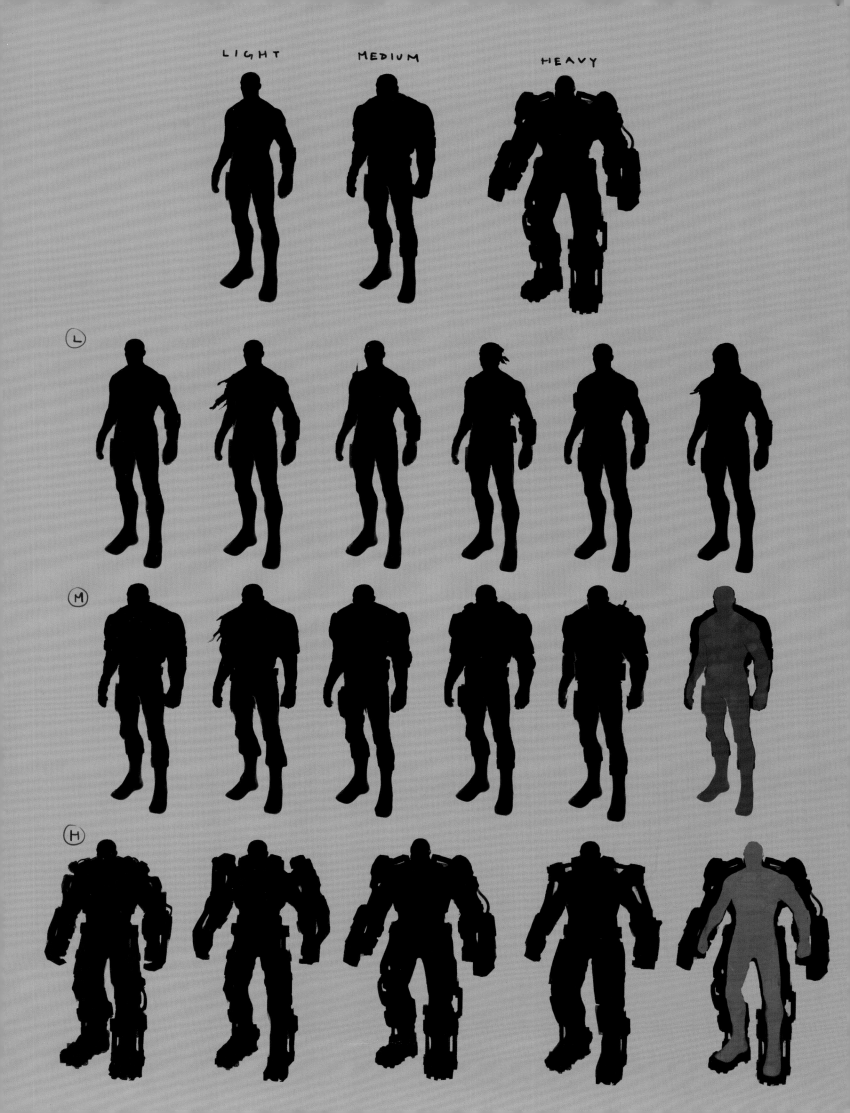

LIGHT   MEDIUM   HEAVY

L

M

H

LIGHT   MEDIUM   HEAVY

"I think that a strong design is always grounded in reality. So we looked at the weapons used by today's soldiers in the battlefield. The more things are based on reality, the easier it is for players to wrap their heads around how they might work and the easier it is to relate to a fictional setting. You are constantly searching for real references that you can pick and choose from. You throw them all in a bag and shake them up and see what comes on top." —SEAMAS GALLAGHER, CONCEPT ARTIST

OPPOSITE: Silhouette studies for Light, Medium, and Heavy armor soldiers. **THIS PAGE:** A Specialist class conventional soldier, with the secondary weapon of the Gremlin.

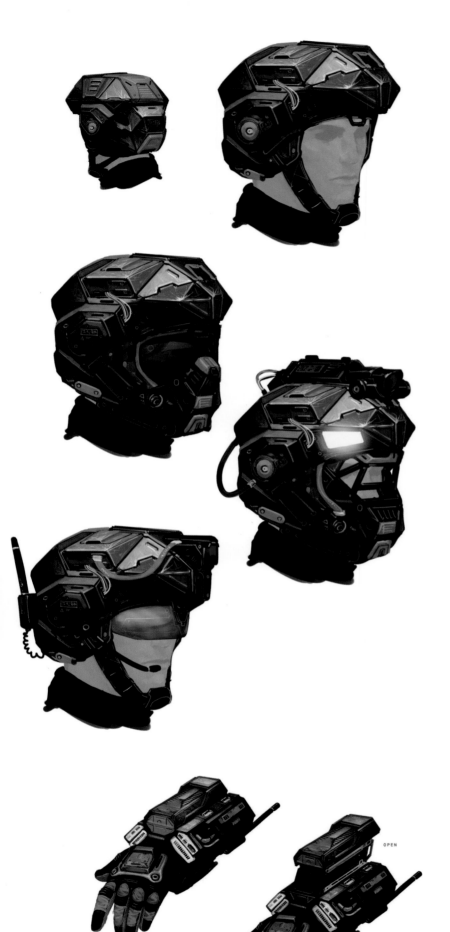

OPPOSITE: Heavy plated armor featuring an exoskeleton. The plating for this armor class is based off of scraps of ADVENT armor technology. **TOP LEFT:** A series of plated helmet concepts with modular parts. **TOP RIGHT:** Light Plated armor study of grappling technology. **LEFT:** A forearm-mounted weapon callout for Heavy Plated armor units. **ABOVE:** Final Medium Plated armor concept. Because this armor is scavenged from ADVENT technology, the development team highlighted asymmetry in these visuals.

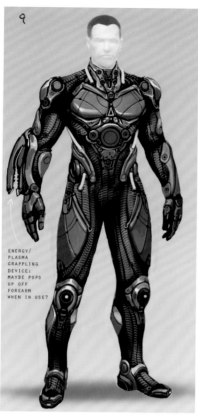

ENERGY/
PLASMA
GRAPPLING
DEVICE:
MAYBE POPS
UP OFF
FOREARM
WHEN IN USE?

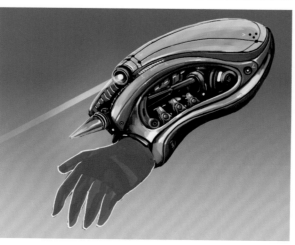

THIS PAGE: Light, Medium, and Heavy Powered armor concepts and color studies, with a callout for a powered grappling hook. **OPPOSITE:** Heavy Powered armor concept. This armor class is much sleeker, stronger, and more advanced than the others.

159

CHAPTER 6

WEAPONS, TECHNOLOGY, & EFFECTS

2 FORWARD LANDING GEARS   1 LARGE MAIN AFT LANDING GEAR

ENGINE

BLACK AREA PART OF ENGINE

2 FORWARD LANDING GEARS   1 LARGE MAIN AFT LANDING GEAR

If there's one motif that consistently drives *XCOM 2*'s art direction, it's believability. That's why when creating the weapons used by the humans to battle the alien overlords, the artists and tech visionaries at Firaxis never strayed too far from what today's military forces utilize in battle. Even when the player gets to experience the high-tech magnetic weapons, a clear visual language is used to signal the way these otherworldly machines operate.

In addition, the weapon upgrades featured in the sequel provided the artists with many opportunities to be creative with the arsenal. "One of the cool things about working with conventional weapons is that they are one of the first things you can upgrade," explains character lead Chris Sulzbach. "The player can basically salvage them off old enemy parts, which you collect through the game. As you get the parts from the ADVENT crew and the alien forces, these upgrades really stand out. They feel dramatically different in terms of their material and shape language: They definitely read alien."

Lead weapon artist David Pacanowski says he also focused on the functionality of the conventional weapons. "They had to feel familiar, so that we could then go crazy with the magnetic weapons," he explains. "There's a definite tiered approach to the weapons: The magnetic ones have more squarish, rectangular shapes while the beam would be the sexy sports car at the end of the tunnel."

Pacanowksi certainly did his homework as he researched for visual resources for the game. "I have always been a fan of both firearms and medieval weapons, but I also hit YouTube and watched a lot of gun-crazy videos. I even bought a Kel-Tec KSG (a bullpup, 12-gauge, pump action) shotgun," he says. "Our tech artists were working with Physically Based Rendering technology, and metal looks great in PBR. It also takes the guesswork out of the visualization. You don't have to worry about different lighting conditions."

"I think that strong design is always grounded in reality," offers concept artist Seamas Gallagher. "We are always pulling from real-world sources, so we really explored what current soldiers are using today. That was a great jumping-off point for us. The more you can ground things in reality, the easier it is for players to wrap their heads around how a weapon might work. It can relate to a fantastic sci-fi setting and still be believable."

Lead effects artist Stephen Jameson was in charge of delivering the game's stunning explosions and depictions of fire. "I had to think of the effects in terms of things we usually don't think of," he says. "For example, when I was working on the fire explosions, I asked myself, 'Okay, if this were an action figure, what would it look like?' Oftentimes it is about taking the elements that are dynamic and interesting, and exaggerating them a bit. The trick is to make something that you'd want to touch if you knew it wasn't going to hurt you!"

Jameson says what really sells the realistic fire effect is the fact that it is made up of large spheres that rise to the top. "The more traditional approach would be to use camera-facing sprites, but our fire and smoke was mostly made up of 3-D spherical meshes—bent out and rotated together as they swirl up through the air," he notes. "Their cohesion, the thickness that comes with using real spheres—that's what makes it work."

Getting very specific with the realism of the visuals is also what gave Jameson a creative edge. "I love working with the *XCOM* art style, which uses strong iconic shapes and emulates the way real explosions and guns work in the real world. It's a stylized universe, but it's not super-simplified and cartoony, which means it depicts the real madness and chaos that are an integral part of a real explosion. You get all the interesting little details that create a naturalistic, almost touchable experience."

PAGES 160–161: A game-resolution render of the Skyranger. **OPPOSITE:** Rough sketches for the Skyranger show how the team envisioned the engine would be situated relative to the landing gear.

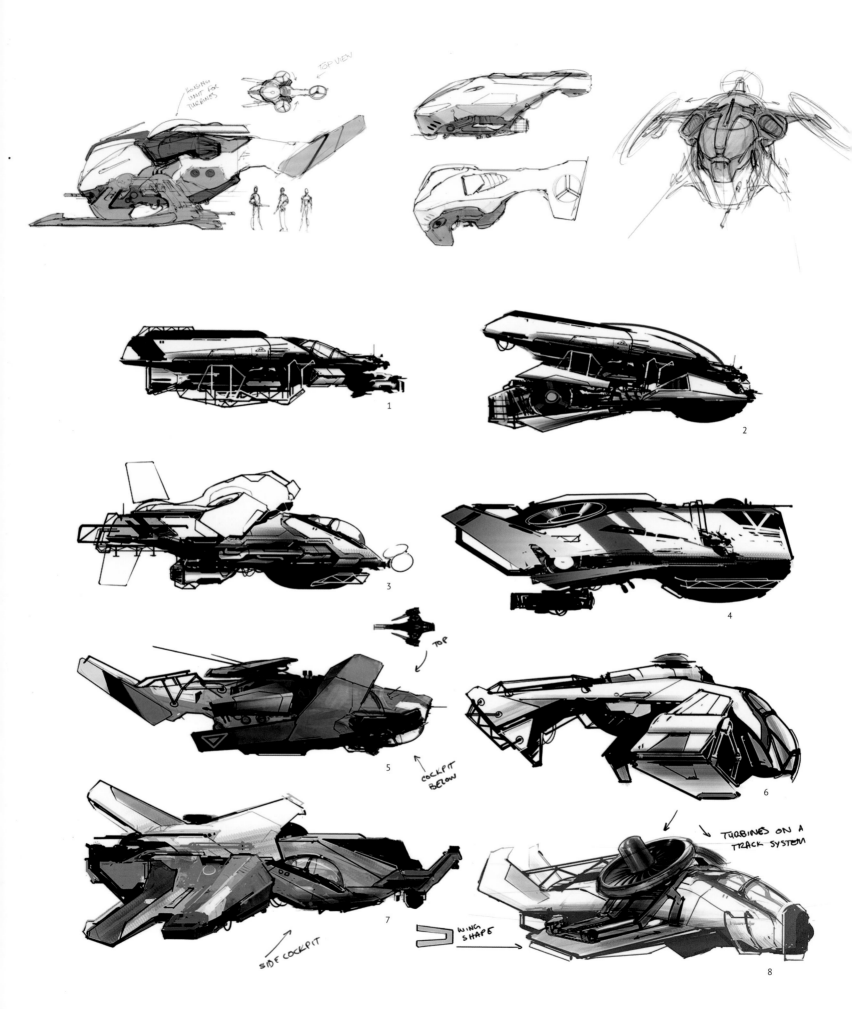

TOP VIEW

HOUSING UNIT FOR TURBINES

TOP

COCKPIT BELOW

SIDE COCKPIT

TURBINES ON A TRACK SYSTEM

WING SHAPE

1

2

3

4

5

6

7

8

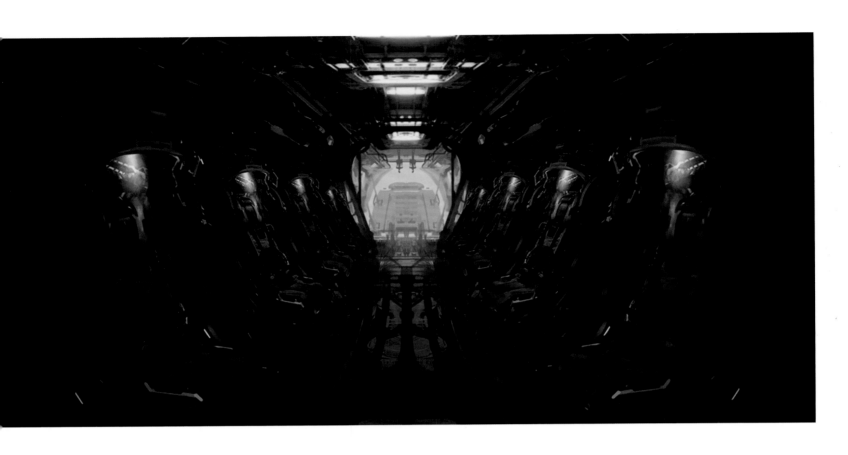

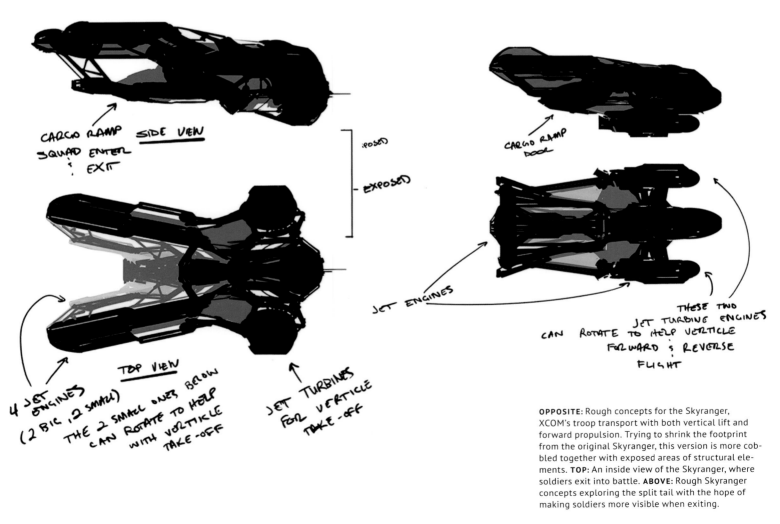

CARGO RAMP SIDE VIEW
SQUAD ENTER & EXIT

CARGO RAMP DOOR

EXPOSED

EXPOSED

JET ENGINES

TOP VIEW

4 JET ENGINES
(2 BIG, 2 SMALL)

THE 2 SMALL ONES BELOW CAN ROTATE TO HELP WITH VERTICLE TAKE-OFF

JET TURBINES FOR VERTICLE TAKE-OFF

THESE TWO JET TURBINE ENGINES CAN ROTATE TO HELP VERTICLE FORWARD & REVERSE FLIGHT

OPPOSITE: Rough concepts for the Skyranger, XCOM's troop transport with both vertical lift and forward propulsion. Trying to shrink the footprint from the original Skyranger, this version is more cobbled together with exposed areas of structural elements. **TOP:** An inside view of the Skyranger, where soldiers exit into battle. **ABOVE:** Rough Skyranger concepts exploring the split tail with the hope of making soldiers more visible when exiting.

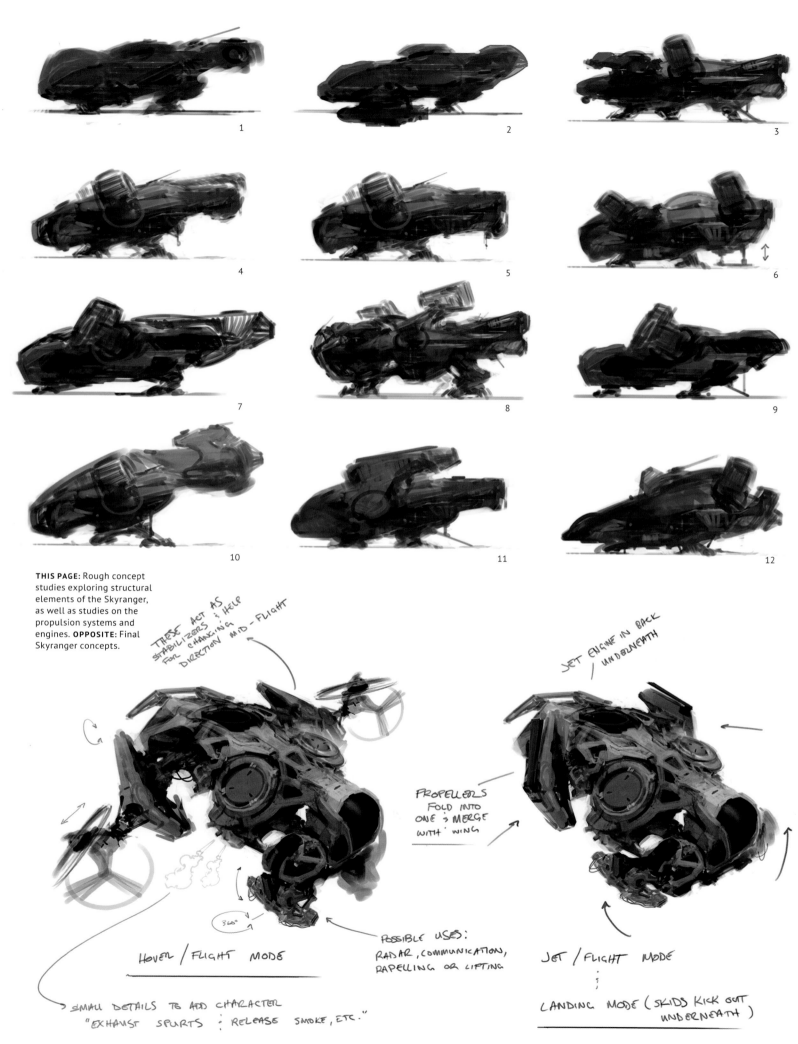

1

2

3

4

5

6

7

8

9

10

11

12

THIS PAGE: Rough concept studies exploring structural elements of the Skyranger, as well as studies on the propulsion systems and engines. **OPPOSITE:** Final Skyranger concepts.

THESE ACT AS STABILIZERS & HELP FOR CHANGING DIRECTION MID - FLIGHT

JET ENGINE IN BACK / UNDERNEATH

PROPELLERS FOLD INTO ONE & MERGE WITH WING

360°

POSSIBLE USES: RADAR, COMMUNICATION, RAPELLING OR LIFTING

HOVER / FLIGHT MODE

JET / FLIGHT MODE
&
LANDING MODE (SKIDS KICK OUT UNDERNEATH)

SMALL DETAILS TO ADD CHARACTER "EXHAUST SPURTS & RELEASE SMOKE, ETC."

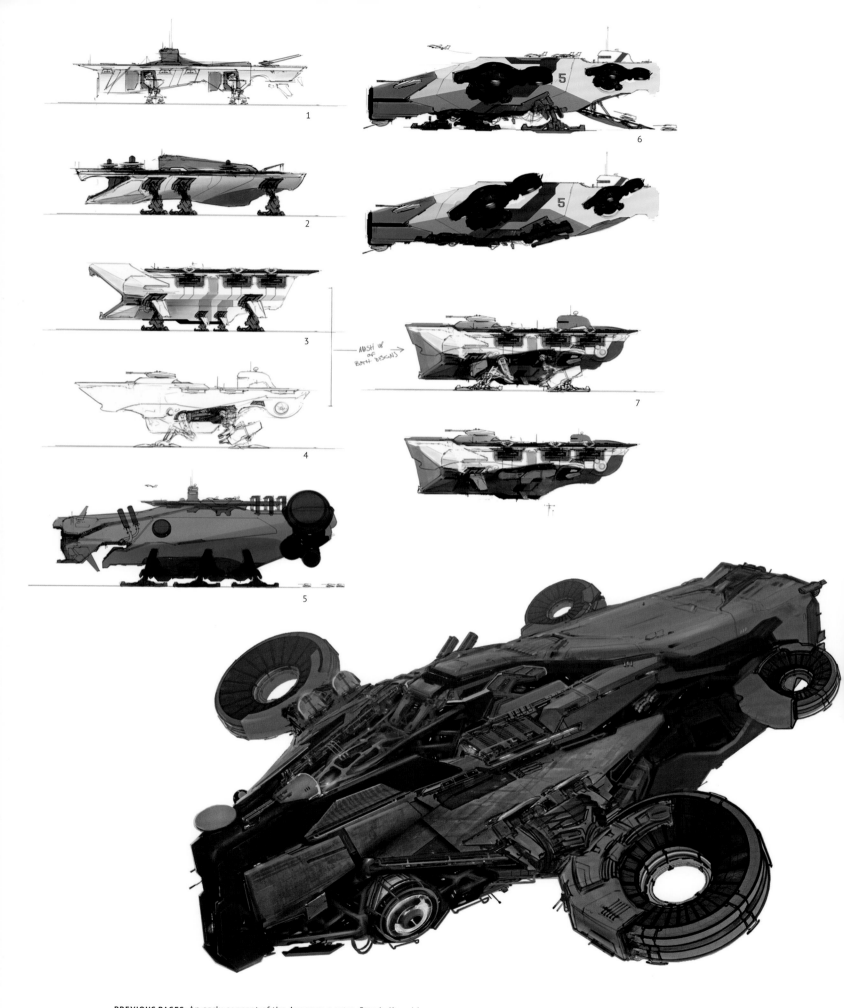

1

2

3

4

5

6

5

MASH UP OF BOTH DESIGNS →

7

5

PREVIOUS PAGES: An early concept of the Avenger, a retro-fitted alien ship that is now XCOM's new flying base. **TOP:** These Avenger concepts are attempts to integrate contemporary naval elements into the profile of the ship. **ABOVE:** Nearly final concept for the exterior of the Avenger. **OPPOSITE TOP:** An early concept showing the underbelly of the Avenger and its landing gear. **OPPOSITE CENTER:** A nearly final concept of the profile for the Avenger. **OPPOSITE BOTTOM:** The initial concepts for the Avenger's silhouette.

E

I

M

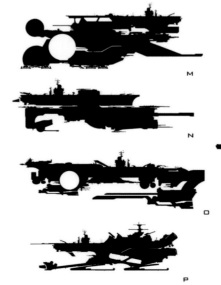

Q

F

J

N

G

K

O

R

H

L

P

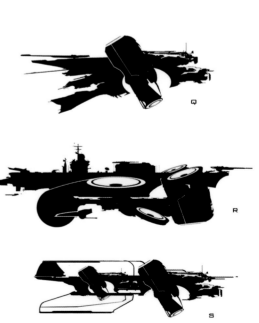

S

"The nice thing about Physical Based Rendering is that it takes the guesswork out of the visualization. You don't have to worry about different lighting conditions. Even all the alien and space materials are based on real life, but we just alter the values to make them stand out." —DAVID PACANOWSKI, LEAD WEAPON ARTIST

LEFT: Interior concept for the armory of the Avenger. This is the room where XCOM soldiers are outfitted and customized. Much like the rest of the ship, there are missing panels and jerry-rigged parts. **TOP:** In-game render of the armory and hangar with the now-smaller Skyranger parked inside. **CENTER:** Interior concept of the Avenger's bridge. This is the nerve center of the vessel and the location for the hologlobe, the heart of XCOM's view on the world. **ABOVE:** An in-game render of the bridge.

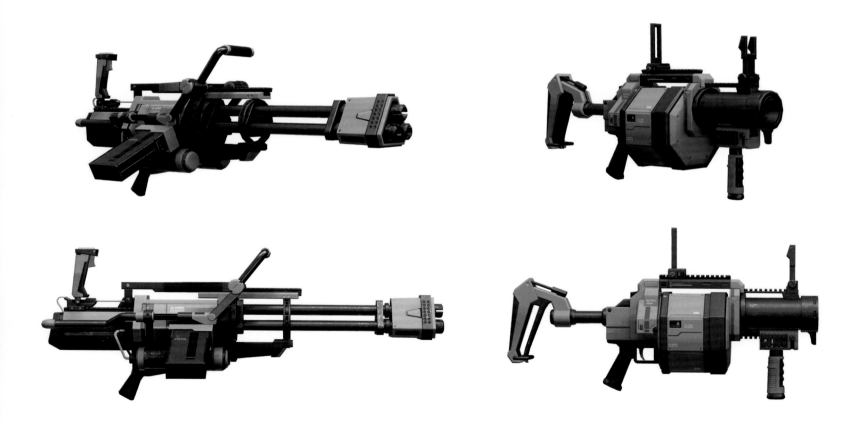

OPPOSITE TOP: Conventional Sniper Rifle concepts, used by XCOM's Sharpshooter class. **OPPOSITE BOTTOM:** Renders of the Cannon and the Grenade Launcher. **TOP:** Concept for the Conventional Cannon, primary weapon for XCOM's Grenadier. **ABOVE:** Early in-game render of the conventional assault rifle, complete with bullets.

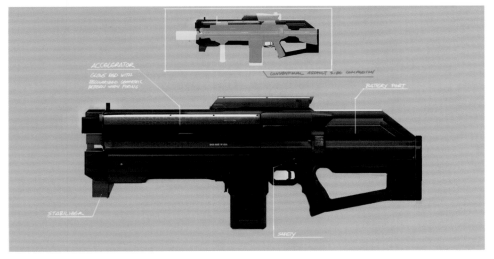

OPPOSITE: In-game renders of ADVENT weapons including the Magnetic Rifle, Magnetic Pistol, and MEC Cannon. **TOP:** Concept for the ADVENT pistol, exclusively carried by the ADVENT Captain. **CENTER:** Concept for the ADVENT Cannon, a weapon only found on the ADVENT MEC. **RIGHT:** An ADVENT Magnetic Rifle concept, a weapon carried by most ADVENT troops.

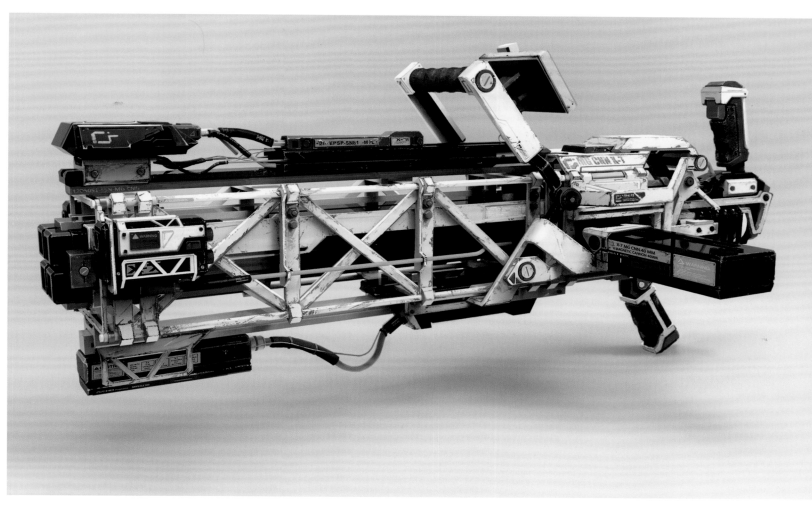

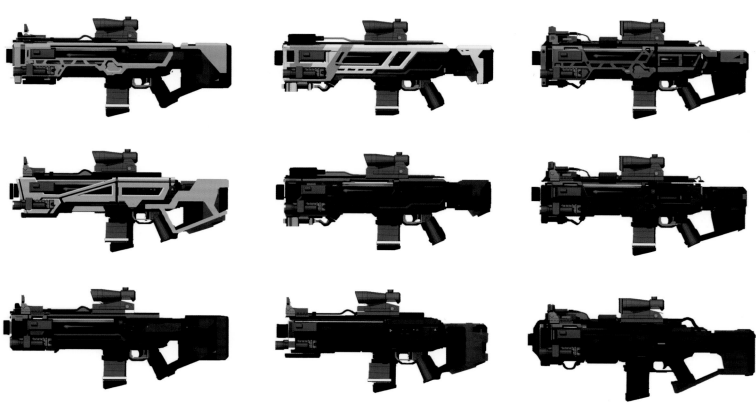

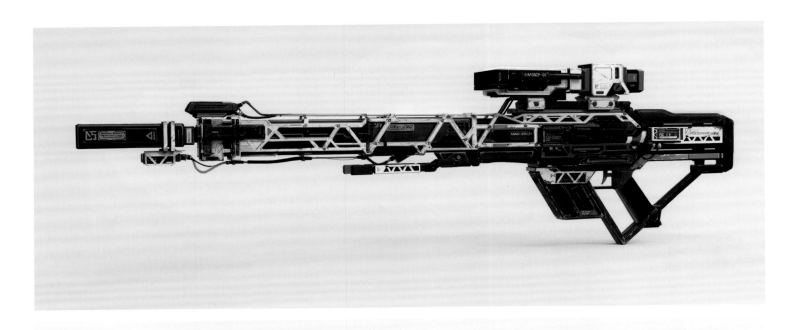

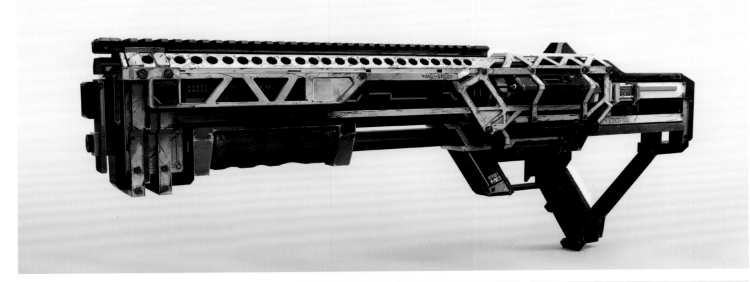

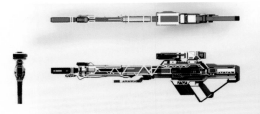

THESE PAGES: Concepts of the range of XCOM Magnetic weapons, showing how the look of this scavenged technology was established.

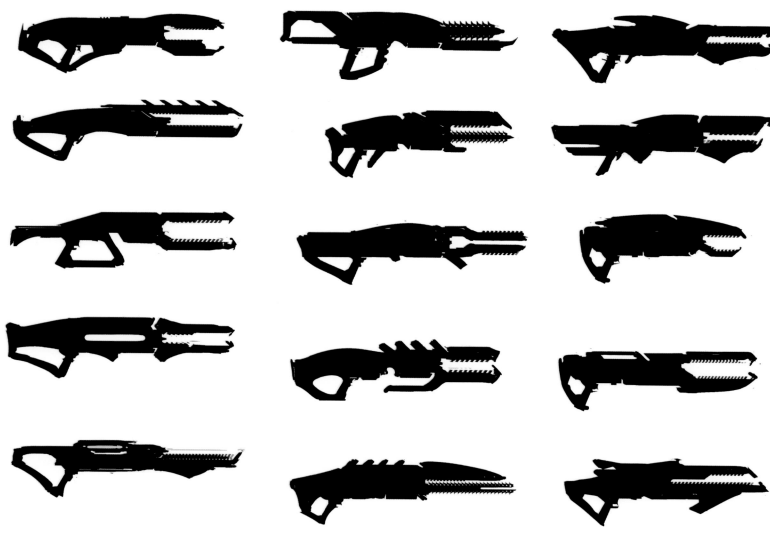

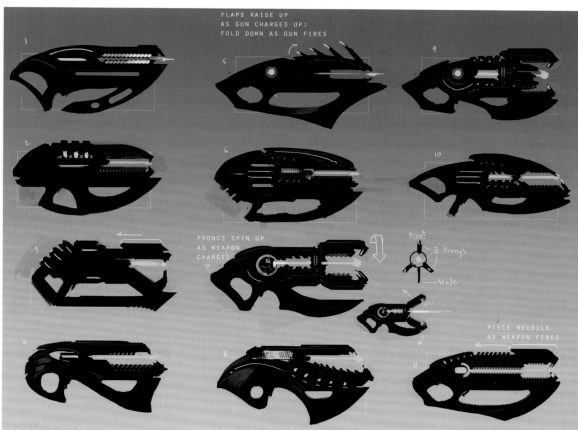

TOP: Silhouette concepts for the Alien Rifle. **RIGHT:** Silhouette concepts for the Alien Cannon. **OPPOSITE TOP:** A Muton Rifle concept complete with melee blade attachment. **OPPOSITE CENTER:** Concepts exploring alien firing mechanism and beam technology. **OPPOSITE BOTTOM:** Alien Assault Rifle concept. This smaller profile weapon is carried by aliens like the Viper.

FLAPS RAISE UP
AS GUN CHARGES UP:
FOLD DOWN AS GUN FIRES

PRONGS SPIN UP
AS WEAPON
CHARGES

Front

3 Prongs

blade

PIECE RECOILS
AS WEAPON FIRES

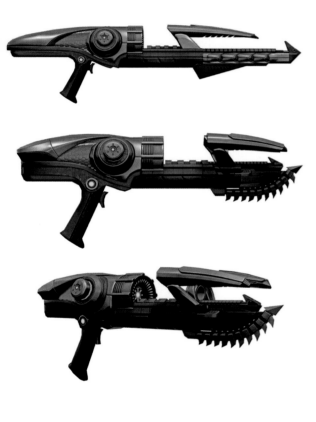

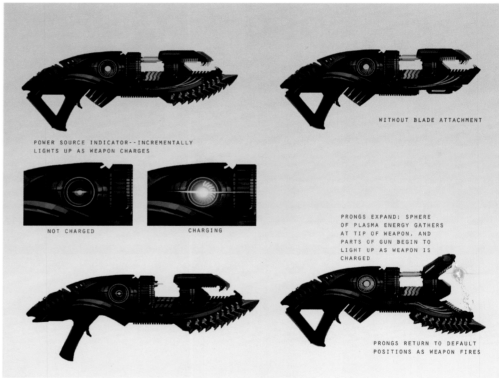

POWER SOURCE INDICATOR--INCREMENTALLY
LIGHTS UP AS WEAPON CHARGES

WITHOUT BLADE ATTACHMENT

NOT CHARGED

CHARGING

PRONGS EXPAND; SPHERE
OF PLASMA ENERGY GATHERS
AT TIP OF WEAPON, AND
PARTS OF GUN BEGIN TO
LIGHT UP AS WEAPON IS
CHARGED

PRONGS RETURN TO DEFAULT
POSITIONS AS WEAPON FIRES

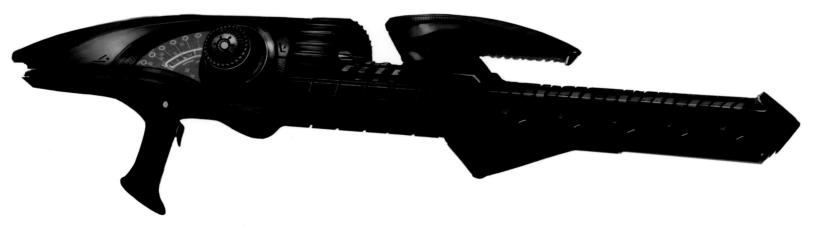

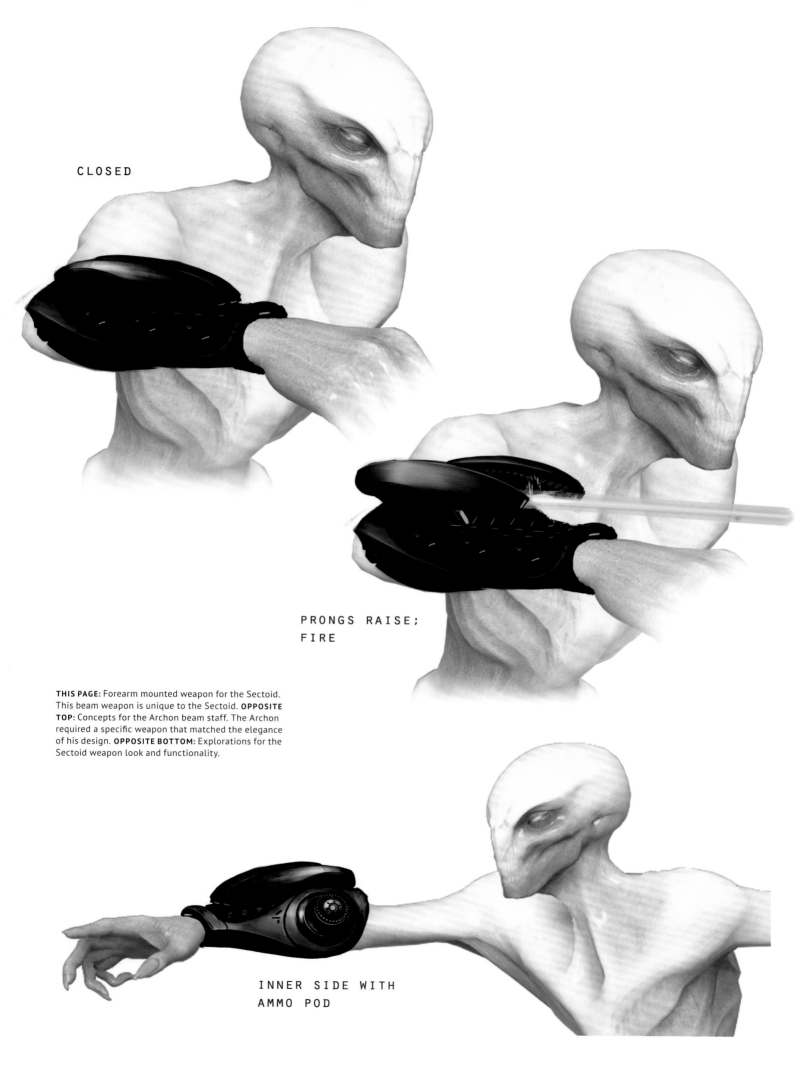

CLOSED

PRONGS RAISE;
FIRE

THIS PAGE: Forearm mounted weapon for the Sectoid.
This beam weapon is unique to the Sectoid. OPPOSITE
TOP: Concepts for the Archon beam staff. The Archon
required a specific weapon that matched the elegance
of his design. OPPOSITE BOTTOM: Explorations for the
Sectoid weapon look and functionality.

INNER SIDE WITH
AMMO POD

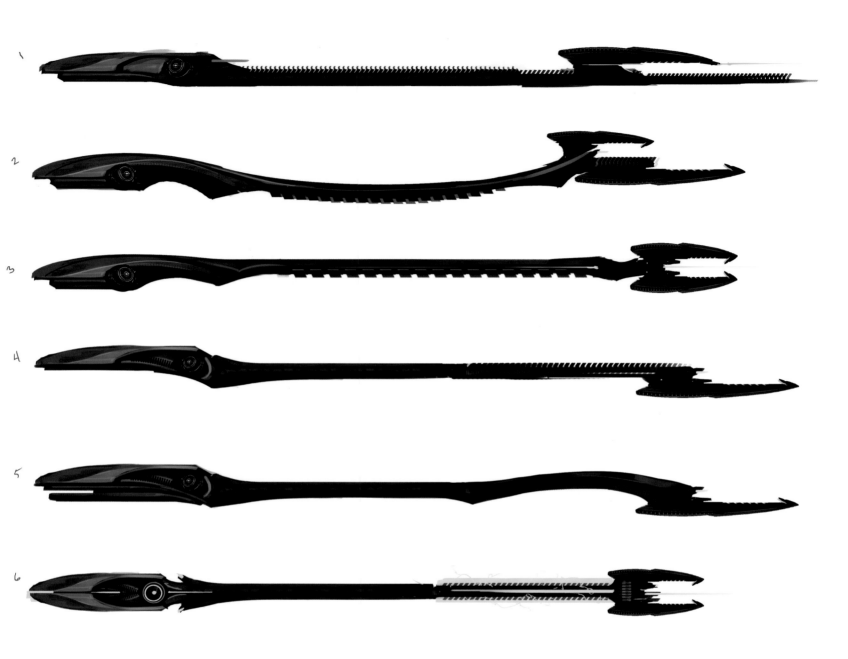

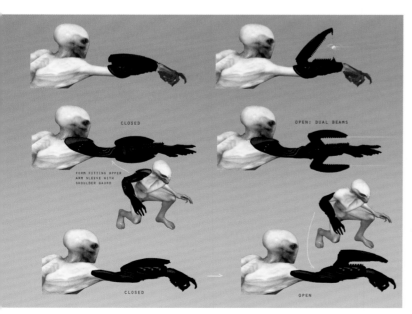

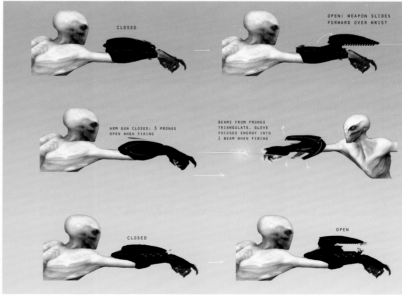

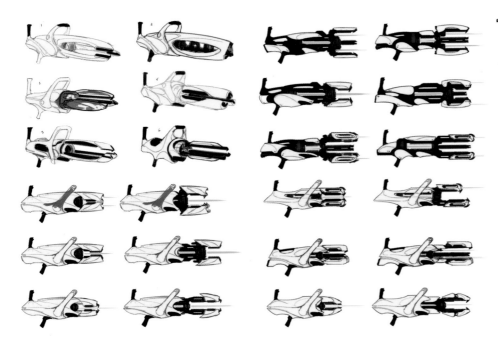

"One of the nice things about the game's conventional weapons is that they're based on reality. The narrative is that you basically salvage upgrades off old enemy parts that you collect through the game. Those upgrades from the ADVENT and the alien forces really stand out. They should feel dramatically different because of their material and shape language, and read very alien."

—CHRIS SULZBACH, CHARACTER LEAD

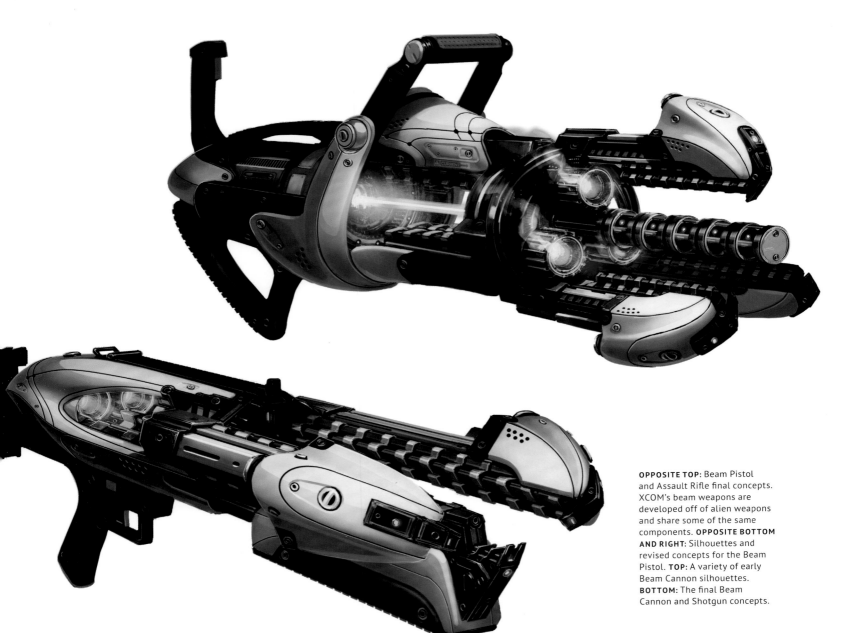

OPPOSITE TOP: Beam Pistol and Assault Rifle final concepts. XCOM's beam weapons are developed off of alien weapons and share some of the same components. OPPOSITE BOTTOM AND RIGHT: Silhouettes and revised concepts for the Beam Pistol. TOP: A variety of early Beam Cannon silhouettes. BOTTOM: The final Beam Cannon and Shotgun concepts.

"The game's conventional weapons should be feel grounded in reality and familiar. Then we can go crazy with the magnetic weapons. We followed a tiered approach to the weapons—the weapons follow a more squarish, rectangular shapes, while the beam would be the sexy sports car at the end of the tunnel."

—DAVID PACANOWSKI, LEAD WEAPON ARTIST

OPPOSITE TOP: The final Beam Sniper Rifle concept, inspired by the smooth lines and shape design of the powered armor. **OPPOSITE BOTTOM:** Early explorations of the Beam Sniper Rifle silhouette. **TOP:** A range of Beam weapons featuring upgraded attachments.

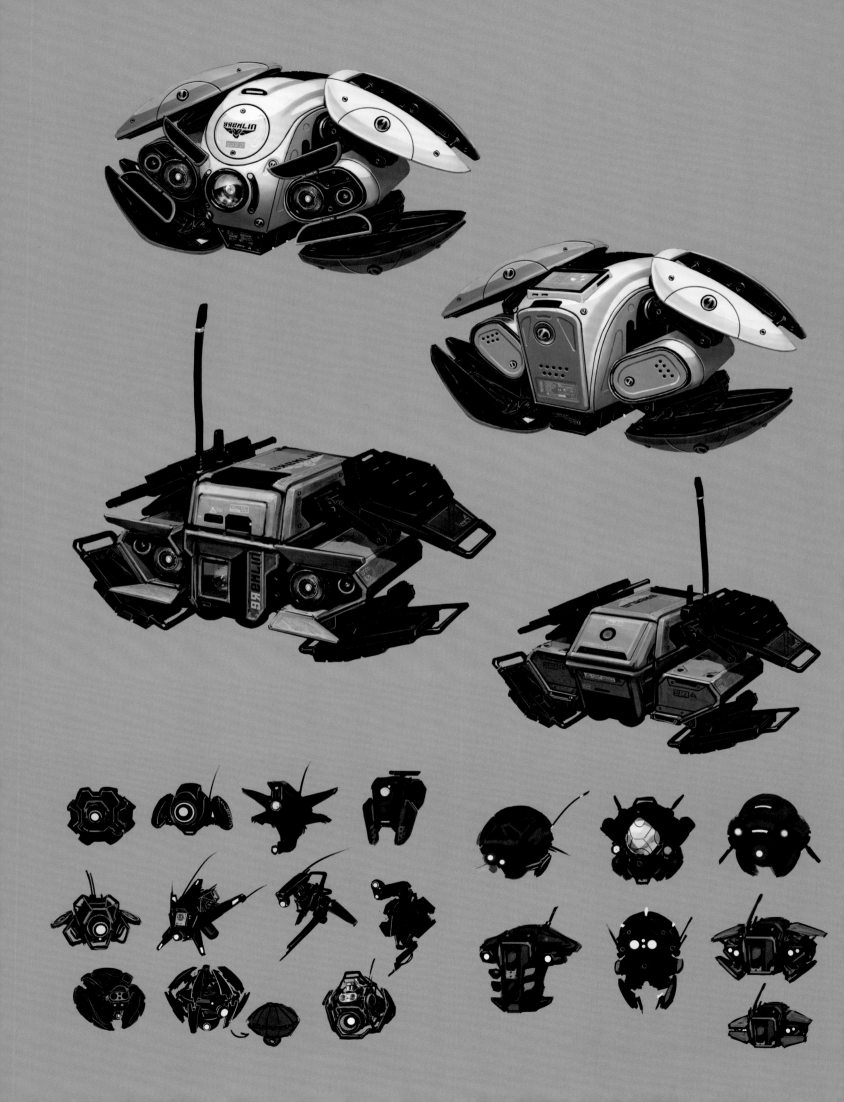

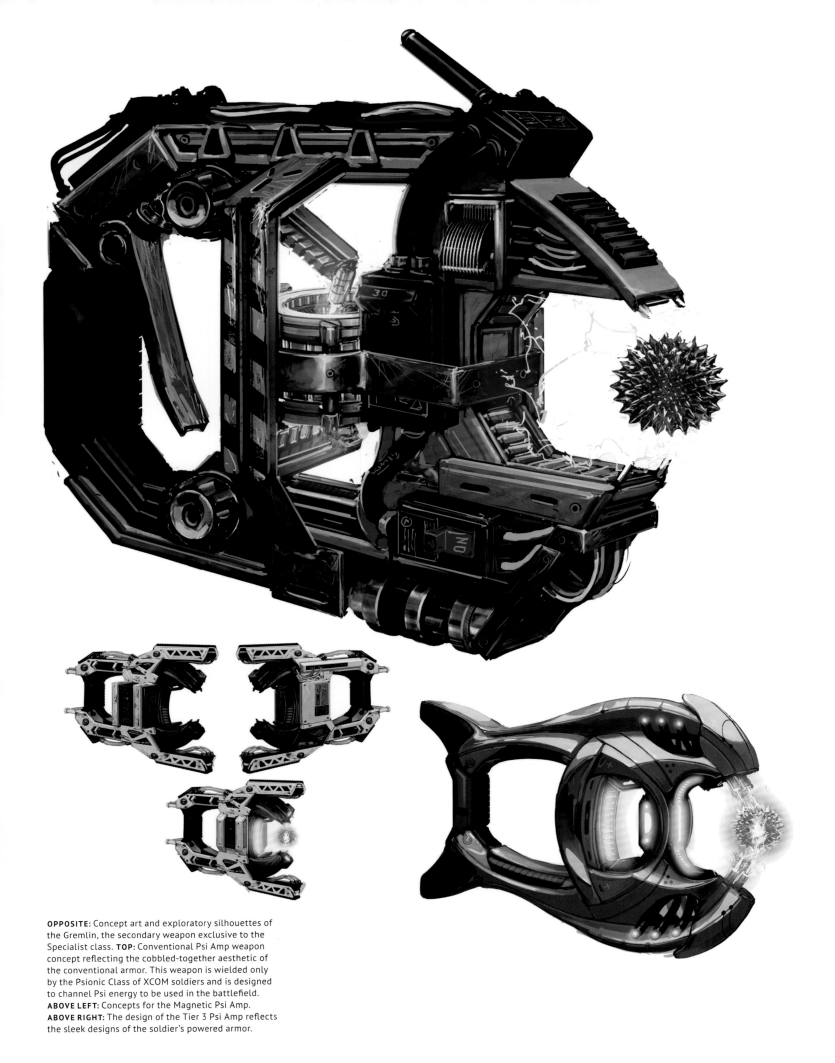

OPPOSITE: Concept art and exploratory silhouettes of the Gremlin, the secondary weapon exclusive to the Specialist class. **TOP:** Conventional Psi Amp weapon concept reflecting the cobbled-together aesthetic of the conventional armor. This weapon is wielded only by the Psionic Class of XCOM soldiers and is designed to channel Psi energy to be used in the battlefield. **ABOVE LEFT:** Concepts for the Magnetic Psi Amp. **ABOVE RIGHT:** The design of the Tier 3 Psi Amp reflects the sleek designs of the soldier's powered armor.

TITAN
BOOKS

A division of Titan Publishing Group Ltd
144 Southwark Street
London SE1 0UP
www.titanbooks.com

Find us on Facebook: www.facebook.com/TitanBooks

Follow us on Twitter: @TitanBooks

Published by Titan Books, London, in 2015.

A CIP catalogue record for this title is available from the British Library.

ISBN: 978-1-78565-124-3

Published by arrangement with Insight Editions, PO Box 3088, San Rafael, CA 94912, USA. www.insighteditions.com

Publisher: Raoul Goff
Acquisitions Manager: Robbie Schmidt
Art Director: Chrissy Kwasnik
Book Design: Dwayne Carter
Additional Design and Layout: Chris Kosek
Executive Editor: Vanessa Lopez
Senior Editor: Ramin Zahed
Associate Editor: Greg Solano
Production Editor: Elaine Ou
Production Managers: Anna Wan & Lina sp Temena

ROOTS of PEACE   REPLANTED PAPER

Insight Editions, in association with Roots of Peace, will plant two trees for each tree used in the manufacturing of this book. Roots of Peace is an internationally renowned humanitarian organization dedicated to eradicating land mines worldwide and converting war-torn lands into productive farms and wildlife habitats. Roots of Peace will plant two million fruit and nut trees in Afghanistan and provide farmers there with the skills and support necessary for sustainable land use.

Manufactured in Hong Kong by Insight Editions

10 9 8 7 6 5 4 3 2 1

PAGES 2–3: Concept art showcases a human being frisked by ADVENT in front of a City Center propaganda statue. **PAGE 6:** The tattered flag of the Resistance. **PAGES 8–9:** An ADVENT propaganda poster. **PAGE 10:** A propaganda poster developed to lure humans to City Centers. **PREVIOUS PAGES:** Concept art showing a member of the Resistance investigating a PSI Gate.